FROM THE FOREWORD

In [*The Wisdom of Wimber: As I See It*], Marty has John speak for himself, adding his own commentary and experiences, bringing John [Wimber] into our early twenty-first century world. ...Remember, John called all of us out of the stands and on to the field, saying, "Everybody gets to play." Suit up and jump in. Marty will help you to find your position.

Don Williams
Author • Pastor • Theologian
Los Angeles, CA

———∞———

Anytime we dig into the Scriptures and find gold, it not only changes us, but it also has the power to change the people around us. Marty is a tried and proven pastor who has given himself to the 'discipling of others' and with this, encouraging the local church. I appreciate Marty's enthusiasm to take John's words of insight and break them down to once again encourage, but also challenge areas of our hearts that can use some 'nudging.'

Christy Wimber
Pastor • Author • Popular Speaker
Yorba Linda, CA

———∞———

This book codifies John Wimber and his theology in a brilliant outline. We have needed something like this for a long time, both as a review for those of us who were there, and an introduction to those who are just getting started in all things kingdom. Way to go Marty!

Bill Jackson
Pastor • Church Historian • Author
Corona, CA

———∞———

This book ought to be indexed under "F" for flamethrower! I predict that as you read it, you won't just be informed. You will also be ignited, as will your experience with Jesus. John Wimber's heart was always bent on igniting hearts to change—to change the church and to change the world. Scripture says, "He makes His angels flames of fire." John loved to play with fire. He was the most effective spiritual "pyromaniac" of his generation. When you read this, you might smell smoke, but don't panic. It's probably just the kindling of your heart being lit again.

Steve Sjogren
Pastor • Life Coach • Author
Claremont, CA

———∿∿∿———

Sometimes, while working on a website, it freezes or just gets stale, and I remember to hit the 'Refresh' icon. The effect is that it uploads fresh insights on the topic at hand. For me, that same effect is evident in what Marty has done with John Wimber's pearls of wisdom. Many people quote John as someone whose teaching they've read, heard, watched on DVD, respected and admired. Boller writes as someone who experienced him as a mentor. Here, teaching is made into wisdom, and observations have been translated into life lessons. Marty has hit the 'Refresh' icon on the Wimber website, in a most honouring way, and with delightful and inspiring results!

Costa Mitchell
Pastor • National Director of
Association of Vineyard Churches Teacher • South Africa

———∿∿∿———

Boller's *The Wisdom of Wimber: As I See It* is a pastor's reflection of John Wimber's winsome theology. This is a book where friends can remember, students can learn, and everyone can be encouraged to "go and play." Go ahead, read it again for the first time.

Winn Griffin
Author • Teacher • Publisher at Harmon Press
Woodinville, WA

The release of *The Wisdom of Wimber: As I See It* is timely. I say this for two reasons. First, as the Vineyard movement ages and a new, younger generation of leaders emerge, we need a way to pass on the best of the founder of our movement to those who did not have the opportunity to know, see, or hear him. Second, as brotherly dialog between different faith-streams increases, it will be helpful to have a volume that introduces those outside the movement to the Vineyard a la John Wimber.

Dave Jacobs
Pastor • Author • Pastoral Coach
Rogue River, OR

THE WISDOM OF WIMBER: AS I SEE IT

FOREWORD BY
DON WILLIAMS

THE
WISDOM
OF **WIMBER**
AS I SEE IT

Christ and His Word
DiscipleshipWorship
EvangelismMission
Compassion Healing
CommunityUnity
Gifts of the Spirit

MARTY BOLLER

HARMON PRESS

Published by:

HARMON PRESS

Woodinville, WA 98077
http://www.harmonpress.com

ISBN: 978-1-935959-55-7
Library of Congress Control Number: 2014946454

Cover Design: Harmon Press

In Memory of John Wimber

Doing his best to make the things
of the kingdom of God real and convincing...
(Acts 19:8, The Message)

Just a fat man from Missouri
who did his very best to get to heaven,
and in the process, taught us the fine art of kingdom living.

DEDICATION

To Sandy Boller

Well, dear one, after nearly forty years of marriage, you finally have a book dedicated to you alone. Thanks for promising me that you'll buy the first copy! But even if you don't, I would still love you with all my heart, soul, and mind for the remainder of our days. Thanks for saying "yes and I do" to this guy back in July of 1975. Outside of my "thing" with Jesus, you're the best-est friend a person could ever have! Love and kisses!

CONTENTS

"Everybody gets to play." Suit up and jump in.

FOREWORD: DON WILLIAMS

Welcome to Wimber, as seen through the lens of Marty Boller. Enough time has passed since John Wimber's death to gain perspective on his unparalleled impact upon and through the twentieth-century church. With well selected quotes from John's writings, organized into ten (10) major concepts of ministry, Marty places Wimber in the world of church growth philosophy, which is all about, in Marty's words, a "three B's ministry" of buildings, budgets and butts (in the pews). Much of this philosophy came historically from the "seeker sensitive" model of Bill Hybels (Willow Creek), where the church is organized and grows as it is programed to meet people's needs. Using the secular corporate model, the church discovered needs then determine the preaching and program of the church. Success in ministry is measured by catering to felt-needs. It's all about people – they determine the church's message and ministry.

Into this culture (and a former shaper of it through his role at Fuller Theological Seminary), came John Wimber. John experienced, along with his wife Carol, what must be described as not only a clear conversion (in John's words, he came "from the pagan pool") and experienced the empowering of the Holy Spirit. In that empowerment, John built a church, which tagged on to the "Jesus Movement" of the late 1960s and '70s. Rather than the church being "seeker sensitive," John's church was about Jesus and his kingdom ministry. If you want to know what this radical church looked like, read Marty's book, cover to cover. You have to do this to get the whole picture.

In our highly transient culture, John estimated that we have people in our churches for three years. In this time we must not only convert them, we must disciple them into maturity in Christ. But how is this to be done? Marty has John speak for himself, adding his own commentary and experiences, bringing John into our early twenty-first century world. One value of this book is that it comes out of Boller's mature, candid reflection and experience in ministry. He helps us to reevaluate John's ministry, as John speaks for himself and Marty reflects. These Wimberisms are hard for any of us to gather. Thank you Marty for doing this work for us.

While appealing to the burned out "buildings, budgets, and butts" leaders, it will open us all up to the radical, enduring message and ministry of John who only desired his work to embody the message and kingdom ministry of Jesus.

Over the years of his ministry, John was committed to church renewal and church planting as the best means of evangelizing the world. His ministry in the United Kingdom brought renewal to a major part of the Church of England. As a result, ministries such as "Soul Survivor" have exploded, bringing thousands of teenagers to Christ. Mike Pilavachi, its leader, reports that at their summer festival in 2014 (originally envisioned by John as "New Wine" festivals for adults), the titular head of the Church of England (Justin Welby, the Archbishop of Canterbury) came and was prayed for (hands on) by thousands of teens. He later gave them the invitation to accept Christ, to which vast numbers responded.

John understated his life, defining it as "just a fat man, trying to get to heaven." However, he was one of the key prophetic visionaries and reformers of the twentieth century church and his work goes on. As you read this book, you will understand why this was and continues to be true. Here is food for your life and direction for your discipleship – whatever form it may take. Remember, John called all of us out of the stands and on to the field, saying, "Everybody gets to play." Suit up and jump in. Marty will help you to find your position.

Don Williams
Author • Pastor • Theologian
Los Angeles, CA

"…just a fat man from Missouri trying to get to heaven."

THE WISDOM OF WIMBER

AS I SEE IT

PREFACE: THE WISDOM OF WIMBER

John Wimber (1934 – 1997) called himself "just a fat man from Missouri trying to get to heaven." On that journey, God allowed John to become a loyal husband, a faithful father, a successful composer/musician, a caring pastor, and a well-known author and speaker who encouraged the whole church of Jesus Christ to draw closer to Jesus, entering into the grace and glory of the ever-expanding kingdom of God. In 1977, John and Carol Wimber planted a church in Yorba Linda, California, that eventually became the birthing place of the Vineyard Church movement, which has now spread into many countries worldwide.[1]

The book you are now reading was originally published in 2014 as a devotional blog series on my website www.pastorboller. com. It is a collection of sixty-four musings on just a handful of writings from John Wimber. Outside of our three-part introduction and one-session conclusion, we have chosen to comment on six Wimber quotes within each of ten themes important to John. They are:

- On Christ and His Word
- On Worship
- On Gifts of the Spirit
- On Community
- On Compassion
- On Healing
- On Mission
- On Unity

- On Evangelism
- On Discipleship

Since the material you will be reading was originally published as a daily blog, you will, on occasion, find a key phrase or thought repeated several times throughout our writings. We decided at the time of editing to keep our material consistent with the original blog format, thus you might find it enjoyable to read our book as a daily devotional, especially since each chapter ends with both a closing prayer and a series of questions for you to ponder.

Happy reading!
In his service,
Marty Boller
October 2014

ACKNOWLEDGEMENTS

I believe it was the great orator for Jesus Christ, Charles H. Spurgeon, who once said that it takes forty years to write a great sermon. If that's the case, now that I'm in my early 60s, following the Master for most of those six decades, I hope I at least have one good book in me! I guess time will tell if *The Wisdom of Wimber: As I See It* will find wings, but I must honestly say, even if it never gets read by many, I know that the journey was well worth it.

There are so many to thank when one writes an appreciation page. Too many, of course, than paper, ink, and fading memory allows. So let me start by giving you just a handful of names. Maybe that will prime the pump of thanksgiving and encourage all of us to be more thankful daily for the special people God brings into our lives as a rich blessing from above.

Winn Griffin: What a joy to work with the wise sage who first edited John Wimber. It's quite the honor (and a bit intimidating, in fact) to work with John's written words, knowing that I'm doing this with one who helped Wimber craft his words in the first place! Your counsel and advice has made this book much, much richer than I could have ever done on my own, and partnering with Harmon Press has been nothing but fantastic!

Dave Jacobs: I tell people who ask, that you, Dave, saved my life. First, as a pastoral coach, and now, as a great friend. I can't tell you how much your input into my life has been used by Jesus to set me on the right path for the remainder of my days. I came to you looking for a coach who would help make me into a church growth rancher. I ended up as a recovering 3-B pastor on my way to becoming a contemplative activist. Not bad, Dave. Not bad, indeed.

Bill Jackson, Costa Mitchell, Steve Sjogren, Christy Wimber and Don Williams: Each of you in your own special way have blessed me beyond words by offering to read this material and then still feel confident enough to write some nice words about it! Thanks for putting your credibility on the line for this old, fat pastor from the Heartland called Iowa. I truly appreciate your kindness, your time, and effort in helping me in this special way.

Okay, that's enough flowers and candy for now. If you're not listed here, it doesn't mean, of course, that I don't appreciate you. All I can say is keep being my friend and I'll put you under serious consideration for Volume 2.

AN INTRODUCTION TO JOHN WIMBER

I'm a fool for Christ. Whose fool are you?

A Fool for Christ

I'm a fool for Christ. Whose fool are you?[2]

L et me begin by first giving you a few facts. It was back in 1984 when the church community my wife, Sandy, and I were a part of, first met up with John Wimber and the group of churches under his leadership called the Vineyard. Our church was called Christ Church of the North Shore at the time and we were a small group of about one hundred or so twenty-something folks assembling in Evanston, Illinois, looking for more of Jesus and finding him as we gathered in his name. The church would later become known as the Vineyard Christian Fellowship of Evanston and grow to become one of the larger churches in the Vineyard movement, sending out dozens and dozens of Jesus-lovers to plant Vineyard churches throughout the world. Sandy and I were one of those many couples that was sent out to plant a Vineyard.

While both Sandy and I had been Christians for much of our lives, this encounter with John Wimber in the 1980s changed our lives forever. John's focus on practicing intimate worship of God, while proclaiming the kingdom message and ministry of Jesus, enthralled us. The power and presence of the Holy Spirit during this season of our lives was absolutely amazing. The simplicity of doing Jesus' stuff and the laid-back, "everybody can play" approach to ministry modeled by Wimber was so inviting, Sandy and I quickly decided to play...and we haven't stopped now for thirty years.

As I see it, here in 2014, thirty years after our first encounters with John, it's time for me to write my personal reflections on some of the many words and works of this great man of God who died in November 1997, just two months before we started our Vineyard church in Cedar Rapids, Iowa.

If I can claim a spiritual father, John Wimber would be that man. Amazingly, our actual contact with one another was very limited. I suppose I spent time with John only three or four times between 1984 and 1997. One of the most memorable was sharing a round of golf with John in Chicago in June of 1986. At one point after viewing one of my typically miserable shots, he turned to me and wryly commented, "Marty, in all my years of golfing, I've never seen anyone play three fare-ways while attempting to play only one hole!" Yet despite the limited contact, John became my mentor over the years and everything in my life (except my golf game!) has been transformed through his. I know that only Jesus Christ can make real-life transformation in a person's life, but for me, I stand amazed at how a simple "fat man who was just trying to get to heaven" was used by our Father to give me so much.

The problem I'm seeing right now is that we have a new generation of church leadership who were never truly exposed to John Wimber and the basic kingdom teachings, which, I believe, can bring vibrant life and healthy understanding to the Christian walk. It's not my desire here to elevate John to sainthood, but simply to give you, as a reader, a taste of John's basic teachings and hopefully keep the messages alive in a new generation.

For those of you who are not familiar with John Wimber, let me briefly introduce him. John Wimber was born in 1934 in Kirksville, Missouri; a little town in northern Missouri, just sixty-five miles from my mom's hometown of Trenton. Growing up in a broken, single-parent home, his maternal grandfather became his father figure, teaching him many much needed lessons he would use throughout his life and ministry. John ended up living most of his life in the Los Angeles basin, pastoring churches in Yorba Linda and Anaheim, California. A talented musician, songwriter, and business man, he was the creative genius behind the Righteous Brothers; a popular musical duo of the 1960s and 70s who made it big when they were signed to be the warm-up band for the Beatles on their first American tour in 1964. Sadly, John never got any of the musical acclaim or riches from the achievements of this well-known duo, since he left the music business immediately upon his radical conversion to Christ in 1963.

In his testimony DVD *I'm a Fool for Christ, Whose Fool Are You?* John tells his poignant story of coming to Jesus plus other vital life stories worthy of your time to listen. Let me close this introduction by recounting for you, in his own words, Wimber's conversion story.

After I had studied the Bible with Gunner Payne (John's spiritual father) for about three months, I could have passed an elementary exam on the cross. I understood there is one God who could be known in three Persons. I understood Jesus is fully God and fully man and he died on the cross for the sins of the world. But I didn't understand that I was a sinner.

I thought I was a good guy. Oh, I knew I had messed up here and there, but I didn't realize how serious my condition was.

But one evening around this time, Carol (John's wife) said to Gunner, "I think it's time to do something about all that we've been learning." Then, as I looked on in utter amazement, she kneeled down on the floor and started praying to what seemed to me to be the ceiling plaster. "Oh God," she said, "I'm sorry for my sin."

I couldn't believe it. Carol was a better person than I, yet she thought she was a sinner. I could feel her pain and the depth of her prayers. Soon she was weeping and repeating, "I'm sorry for my sin."

There were six or seven people in the room, all with their eyes closed. I looked at them and then it hit me: *They've all prayed this prayer too!* I started sweating bullets. I thought I was going to die.

The perspiration ran down my face, and I thought, "I'm not going to do this. This is dumb. I'm a good guy."

Then it struck me. Carol wasn't praying to the plaster; she was praying to a person, to a God who could hear her. In comparison to him, she knew she was a sinner in need of forgiveness.

In a flash, the cross made personal sense to me. Suddenly I knew something that I had never known before: I had hurt God's feelings. He loved me and in his love for me he sent Jesus. But I had turned away from that love; I had shunned it all of my life. I was a sinner, desperately in need of the cross.

Then I too was kneeling on the floor, sobbing, nose running, eyes watering, every square inch of my flesh perspiring profusely. I had this overwhelming sense that I was talking with someone who had been with me all of my life, but whom I had failed to recognize. Like Carol, I began talking to the living God, telling him that I was a sinner. About the only words I could say aloud were, "Oh God! Oh God! Oh God!"

I knew something revolutionary was going on inside of me. I thought, "I hope this works, because I'm making a complete fool of myself." Then the Lord brought to mind a man I had seen in Pershing Square in Los Angeles a number of years before. He was wearing a sign that said, "I'm a fool for Christ. Whose fool are you?" I thought at the time, "That's the most stupid thing I've ever seen." But as I kneeled on the floor, I realized the truth of the odd sign: the cross is foolishness "to those who are perishing" (1 Cor. 1:18).

That night I knelt at the cross and believed in Jesus. I've been a fool for Christ ever since.[3]

PRAYER

Each of these sections will close with a prayer that you can pray or if you choose to pray your own prayer, giving thanks for those women and men whose shoulders you stand on as you continue your journey.

Thank you, Lord, for the way you use the testimonies and lives of others who have gone before me to encourage me in my own personalized, spiritual journey. Thank you, Jesus, for the life of John Wimber, which was used in such powerful ways in helping me grow in you. For your name's sake. Amen!

QUESTIONS FOR YOU TO PONDER

- What would it look like for me to become "a fool for Christ?"
- Am I confident enough in the Lord's ability to lead and guide me?
- Am I secure enough in his love to trust that his ways are far higher and much better than mine?
- Am I brave enough to let go of what others might think of

me so I can truly follow the Spirit wherever and whenever he may lead?

So, what is God speaking to you today as you ponder the *Wisdom of Wimber?*

DOIN' THE STUFF

....

When do we get to do the stuff?[4]

....

Ibelieve that John Wimber was the founding father of what is, today, called the Association of Vineyard Churches; a worldwide movement now embracing over 1,500 churches worldwide.

In the late 60s and early 70s, the Jesus Movement was in full gear and countless young men and women across the USA were being drawn into loving relationships with Jesus of Nazareth. Southern California had become a hotbed for God-activity at the time, rock-n-roll was changing the music scene, and by the early 1970s, newly saved musicians were writing and recording music that would eventually transform everything we called church music. Radically saved artists like Keith Green and others joined with Kenn Gulliksen and the Vineyard and suddenly, an excitement to plant new Vineyard churches for new, younger Christians was ablaze. Into that scene, in 1975 a young church planter named Kenn Gulliksen brought together seven church communities that he had planted to form the Vineyard.[5] About this same time, Kenn met John and Carol Wimber. The Wimbers and a handful of their friends were Quakers, living in and around Anaheim, California. Like so many other mainline churches at the time, the charismatic movement had rocked their little Quaker church in Yorba Linda with an explosive move of the Holy Spirit.

John had been serving in Yorba Linda as a lay leader and then as co-pastor since his radical conversion to Christ[6] in 1963. Under Wimber's leadership, their Friends Church grew dramatically, with much of that growth coming from John's personal commitment to sharing his faith with everyone he met. In 1974, Wimber enrolled in a Peter Wagner course at Fuller Seminary. Wagner was a theoretician of Church Growth and he knew that Wimber was a practitioner. Wagner and Wimber teamed up when Wagner called to offer him a job to establish the Fuller Institute of Evangelism and Church Growth.[7] During much of the 1970s, Wimber traveled extensively around the USA and Canada, working with pastors and church leaders in church growth and ministry development. It was in this role, God began exposing him to a broader spectrum of Christianity, encouraging him to love and appreciate the presence of God as it manifested throughout the larger church across North America.

In 1976, Jesus began encouraging John to leave his job at Fuller and return to day-to-day pastoral ministry back home in Yorba Linda. By 1977, a new church was formed, but this time, the church John pastored would be governed outside the framework of the Quaker denomination. After being asked to leave the Friends Church because of their charismatic experiences, John and Carol joined forces with the Calvary Chapel movement under the direction of Chuck Smith. It was during this season that Kenn Gulliksen approached John, asking him to join him, bringing Wimber's church planting expertise to the movement. By 1982, a total transition in leadership had occurred, with Kenn humbly laying down his leadership role with Vineyard, turning it over completely to John.

It's important to mention here that early in Wimber's journey with Christ, John learned from his Quaker mentor, Gunner Payne, that the Bible was the source of all truth when it came to knowing and experiencing God. Later on in life, John often said of himself that he was, at the time of his conversion, a "beer-guzzling, drug-abusing pop musician, who was converted at the age of twenty-nine while chain-smoking my way through a Quaker-led Bible study."

Crediting his Quaker mentor, Wimber became a hungry Christian, dedicating himself to the reading and application of God's Word. Under Gunner's leadership, John became enthralled with the Scriptures. Finally, after several weeks of reading about the life-changing miracles found throughout the Bible, he became curious that much of what he was reading about was not being found at the church he was attending. Christy Wimber tells the story this way:

> Shortly after John became a Christian, he became a voracious

Bible reader. The Scriptures excited him, and finally after reading for weeks about life changing miracles in the Bible and attending boring church services, John asked one of the lay leaders, "When do we get to do the stuff?"

"What stuff?" asked the leader.

"You know the stuff here in the Bible, the stuff Jesus did like healing the sick, raising the dead, healing the blind. You know, stuff like that!"

"Well, we don't do that anymore." the man said to John.

To which John replied, "You don't? Then what do you do?"

"Well, we do what we did here this morning." the man replied.

John answered, "You mean I gave drugs up for that?"[8]

This frustrating conversation back in the mid-1960s started Wimber on a biblically based pursuit of Jesus and his kingdom-driven, world-changing, people-loving ministry. The pursuit of "doin' the stuff" honestly, cost him a lot later in life. Over time, because of his relentless pursuit to follow the words and works of Christ, John, in later years, lost his career at Fuller, his pastoral position in several different churches, and eventually much of his reputation amongst many of his evangelical Christian friends.

Yikes. I guess when you are serious about following Jesus, doin' his stuff can be costly! More on that in chapters to come!

PRAYER

Father, I confess that I share in John Wimber's frustration. Church life across America seems to be focused exclusively on ministry development, creative programming, and the entertainment and edification of the saints. Holy Spirit, give me a holy frustration to move away from standardized American church life so that I might be more actively involved with the actual stuff Jesus did in his ministry. For your name's sake. Amen!

QUESTIONS FOR YOU TO PONDER

- Do both my theology and my approach to missions need a wake-up call from Jesus?

- Have I become increasingly complacent; being content to preach and teach about Jesus' amazing ministry, but never actually attempting to do the stuff Jesus and his followers actually did?

So, what is God speaking to you today as you ponder the *Wisdom of Wimber?*

BEING BIBLICALLY OBEDIENT

It's not enough to be biblically literate; we must also learn to be biblically obedient![9]

So what exactly did Wimber mean when he encouraged people toward biblical obedience?

As we just discussed, it was early in his journey with Jesus when he realized that it was vitally important for him, as a fledging follower of Christ, to obey those things he was reading in God's Word. For example, when John read Jesus' words in John 14:15; "If you love me, keep my commands," he took it seriously. And when Jesus told his disciples in the Great Commission (Matthew 28), "therefore go and make disciples of all nations...teaching them to obey *everything* I have commanded you," John Wimber actually believed that *everything* meant *all* of the things the Master asked his first century disciples to do!

So in Wimber's mind, the phrase 'doin' the stuff' was defined by *all* of the activity we find Jesus saying and doing in the gospels.

At a pastor's conference in July, 1991, Wimber taught on ten areas of ministry that he believed to be essentials for any church who wants to be a "doin' the stuff" kind of church. At that conference, he listed ten focused themes he termed as a Genetic Code for churches who wanted to be God-worshipping, Jesus-centered, Spirit-directed communities, set apart for the kingdom purposes of God. Let me share these ten common denominators, in John's words:

1. Clear, accurate biblical teaching.
2. Contemporary worship in the freedom of the Spirit.
3. The gifts of the Spirit in operation.
4. An active small group ministry.
5. Ministry to the poor, widows, orphans, and those who are broken.

6. Physical healing with special emphasis on signs and wonders as seen in the Book of Acts.
7. A commitment to missions: church planting at home and world missions abroad.
8. Unity within the whole body of Christ, a relationship with other local churches.
9. Evangelistic outreach.
10. Equipping the saints in areas such as discipleship, ministry, serving, giving, finances, family, etc.

As I was preparing this book, I decided to take Wimber's Genetic Code, re-word it just a bit, and place some of John's richest quotes under each of these ten themes. So as we go along, you'll find these ten headers leading our way. They are:

- On Christ and His Word
- On Worship
- On Gifts of the Spirit
- On Community
- On Compassion
- On Healing
- On Mission
- On Unity
- On Evangelism
- On Discipleship

So, ready or not, here we go. Thanks John Wimber, for all you gave us. As we recount some of your best thoughts, may the Lord enrich us, just as he did back in the day.

PRAYER

Father, I confess that it's much easier for me to be biblically literate than it is to be biblically obedient. Wimber was right, Lord. I must learn to yield not only my mind to you, making sure I'm doctrinally sound; but I also need to yield my time, energy, and resources so that my entire life is fully obedient to all Jesus' commands of me. For your name's sake. Amen!

QUESTIONS FOR YOU TO PONDER

- What might it look like for me to act with complete obedience on all of the truths I find in Scripture?
- If simply believing in Jesus' words is not enough, what might it look like for me to become pro-actively involved with *everything* Jesus commands of his followers?
- What would it look like for me to become a "doer" of Jesus' stuff?

So, what is God speaking to you today as you ponder the *Wisdom of Wimber?*

ON CHRIST AND HIS WORD

"I'm just a coin in the Lord's pocket,..."

JESUS' KINGDOM MINISTRY

John, I've seen *your* ministry, and now I'd like to show you *mine!*[10]

John Wimber modeled for me the fine art of living and ministering in the kingdom life of Jesus Christ. Yet when one asked Wimber about himself, he'd often reply, "Hey...I'm just a fat man from Missouri trying my very best to get to heaven!" Folks would always laugh at that line, but quite honestly, John knew full well that his salvation came only by the grace of the Lord and not by anything of worth that he had accomplished in his life or ministry. This was his way of identifying himself as being like everyone else. He did not see himself as special.

John would often say, "I'm just a coin in the Lord's pocket," "Jesus can spend me and my life in any fashion he would like." Before his untimely death in November of 1997, this ordinary man of faith, one simple coin in the Lord's pocket, had been raised up as an international speaker, a best-selling author, pastor of the Vineyard Christian Fellowship in Anaheim, California, and founder of the Vineyard Movement worldwide.

Wimber first gave his life to Christ in 1963 and when he did, he quickly learned that the way of life to which he was accustomed needed to die so that he could learn to walk in the kingdom ways of God.

And while you'd think that this turning away from our earthly ways to live in God's higher ways is a lesson reserved for new believers, Wimber was quick to admit that every step of his journey with Jesus was filled with a continual awareness that his thoughts were not like God's, nor were his ways always compatible with the way the Holy Spirit was leading. John used to put it this way... "The way in (humbling oneself before the Lord for salvation) is the way on (humility being the key to successful discipleship)."

Wimber served a dozen years in full-time ministry, successfully pastoring a local church in the Los Angeles basin, followed by several years traveling throughout North America, working for Fuller Evangelistic Association where he helped pastors from a variety of denominational backgrounds grow their churches. In 1976 with all this ministry activity, he found himself burned out and weary; tired of working with what author Eugene Peterson calls "the Americanized church." In his testimony DVD, *I'm A Fool For Christ, Whose Fool Are You?* Wimber explains that he had reached a point in ministry in 1976 where it no longer tasted like it once did. He enjoyed being used by God in encouraging pastors and local churches in the things of God, but personally he had run himself ragged, worn down to a threadbare spiritual existence.

One night in the spring of 1976 in a hotel room in Detroit, Michigan, John opened the Bible and began to read it for himself. Unfortunately, he had allowed his church growth ministry to become so consuming, he had, for several years running, been opening the Bible daily, but only for others, never for himself. This pivotal evening in the Motor City, God changed all that.

As he read from the Psalms, crying out to God for a dramatic change in his hopeless situation, he fell asleep. Suddenly, as he was lying there on his hotel bed, the Lord began speaking to him. While he claimed it was not an audible voice, it was loud enough to wake him up.

"John, I've seen *your* ministry." the Lord began.

As he told the story, he suggested that the Lord wasn't speaking to him in a mean tone or in a way meant to be critical, but simply in a way that told him that while Jesus appreciated his many efforts in ministry, the fruit had not been all that impressive!

"John, I've seen *your* ministry (pregnant pause)…and *now* I'd like to show you *mine!*"

As he heard this, he broke into a time of deep sobbing. The thought of laying down his own ministry to step into Jesus' ministry was overwhelmingly joyful to him. The idea that he didn't need to get up in the morning and make something good happen for the cause of Christ was life-giving, to say the least. The truth that Jesus has a pre-existing ministry, which was already in-place and in-process, and all John had to do was watch for it and join Jesus where he was already working, was absolutely revolutionary.

And you know what, dear friends? This concept of Jesus asking us pastors and ministry overseers to stop doing our own ministry so that we might join him with his is *still* absolutely revolutionary!

I wonder when twenty-first century pastors, teachers, elders, deacons, overseers, and the like, will learn the same Isaiah 55 lesson John learned back in Detroit in 1976?

"For my thoughts are not your thoughts,
   neither are your ways my ways,"
      declares the LORD.
"As the heavens are higher than the earth,
   so are my ways higher than your ways
and my thoughts than your thoughts" (Isaiah 55: 8-9).

As it turned out, this one word from God turned Wimber's life and ministry around drastically. Everything changed for him after that night in a Detroit hotel room when God spoke a hard truth to one of his faithful servants. From this point forward, he knew in his heart that he no longer had a ministry belonging to him, but simply an assignment from the Master calling him to follow in obedience, placing his hands and feet only where Jesus asked him.

Maybe it's time we re-apply this same powerful truth into *our lives* and *his ministry* here in the first part of the twenty-first century? What say you?

"I've seen *your* ministry, (fill in your name)...and now I'd like to show you *mine!*" Jesus of Nazareth.

PRAYER

Jesus, I quickly confess that *my* life and ministry can become all consuming; many times at the cost of losing track of *you!* Father, when that happens, I ask that you will always send a messenger to me, like you did to John Wimber, reminding me that I, quite honestly, don't have a ministry and that only Jesus does. Spirit, empower me to always pursue the kingdom ministry of Jesus over and above my own. For your name's sake. Amen!

QUESTIONS FOR YOU TO PONDER

- How have I fallen prey to the consuming interests and constant demands of keeping my life and ministry alive and well?
- What might it look like to lay down my interests, decreasing my influence and demands, while preferring and deferring to Jesus and the advancing kingdom ministry of God?

So what is God speaking to you today as you ponder the *Wisdom of Wimber?*

CHRIST-CENTEREDNESS

My hope is that the Vineyard remains a Christ-centered group focused on the main teachings of Scripture as we follow Augustine's ancient advice: "In essentials unity, in non-essentials diversity, in all things charity." We are thankful for the ideas God calls us to implement. If they are solid, it is because they are his and rooted in rock solid Scripture, in tune (at least in part) with some of what the Holy Spirit is doing today. And though the Vineyard is a mere thread in the global tapestry of the church, I believe it is a thread of his weaving. May God always empower us to continue Jesus' ministry![11]

In 1976, just prior to the days when John and his wife, Carol, started their new church plant in Yorba Linda, he had a massive shift in the way he viewed ministry. Up until the time the Lord spoke to him (see the previous section), he believed that ministry was something we did for God. But after his encounter with Jesus in that hotel room in Detroit in 1976, he knew that he would never have a ministry of his own ever again.

"There's only *one* ministry out there," John would tell pastors. "It's *Jesus'* ministry!"

I can still hear John telling pastors that if they've come to him to "find" their ministries or to improve their ministry, then they've come to the wrong place. In his mind, a leader's job was never to work on finding your own ministry, but to discover what Jesus was doing in his ministry and then quickly run to involve ourselves with *that*.

As I see it, ever since his encounter with the Lord in 1976, Wimber became obsessed with finding and doing the ministry that belonged to Jesus of Nazareth. And while that sounds really noble, it also can ruin you.

Why? Because being Christ-centered, focusing exclusively on

29

the words and works of Jesus of Nazareth, giving yourself completely to the things of the Lord, means there's little to no wiggle room left for our own personal agendas. And quite honestly, it's been my personal experience over the years, that once I make that conscious choice to never have a ministry of my own, Jesus will often come to me, reminding me of that commitment whenever I tend to step over the line, trying to make things happen out of my own strength!

Christ-centeredness, you see, literally means Jesus is in the middle while I go off to the side. Now, keep in mind, that being off to the side in Jesus' presence is still a beautiful thing. I've found that whenever I'm successful in becoming a sidebar to Jesus' ministry, it's actually much more fun (and productive!) than when I'm trying to build a ministry myself!

Hmm.

I wonder if that's why Jesus was so successful in everything he did? I wonder if Jesus learned the fine art of deferring to God the Father and his ministry, rather than trying his best to make something happen on his own?

Wait! I remember. Jesus said it himself.

> Very truly I tell you, the Son can do nothing by himself; he can do only what he sees his Father doing, because whatever the Father does the Son also does. (John 5: 19)

Interesting, isn't it?

Jesus, the God-man from Nazareth, who now has the *only* ministry in town, had to arrive there by doing the same thing that he is asking us to do: Prefer and defer to God. Bow in adoration before the Holy One and follow Yahweh in humble obedience. Lay down my rights to defer to God's right to rule and reign.

Not bad advice, John.

Christ-centeredness in all we do. I think that one will still preach well here in our self-centered, self-motivated, self-edifying, self-glorifying culture, don't you?

PRAYER

Father God, I confess that learning to prefer and defer to you is not an easy task. Learning to wait on you, looking and listening for those things you are doing before I initiate my own agendas is obviously a fine art that Jesus practiced throughout his life. Holy Spirit, indwell me and empower me to live in a like manner, learning to do and say only those things I see Jesus doing. For your name's sake. Amen!

QUESTIONS FOR YOU TO PONDER

- How would true Christ-centeredness change the way I've arranged my life?
- What needs to change in my approach to life and ministry, so that I lay down my personal agendas, preferring and deferring to the one ministry that changes everything, the ministry of Jesus?

So what is God speaking to you today as you ponder the *Wisdom of Wimber?*

BEING WITH JESUS

Yes, I want loyalty, but at this point of my life, I'm trying to carefully take tentacles off *me* and put them *on the Lord*. I see this
as essential if there's going to be a Vineyard after John Wimber.

He appointed twelve—designating them apostles--that
they might be with him and that He might send them out
to preach and to have authority to cast out the demons.
(Mark 3:14-15)

Notice the phrase, "*that they might be with him.*" You're called to
Jesus. Jesus was, and is, the only disciple-maker. We make disciples in the sense that we work with the people who are being
called to be *his* disciples. But the ultimate loyalty and commitment belongs to him. [12]

A disciple is one who follows another person's life very closely. A disciple consciously chooses to stick close to another
person, learning just about everything one can learn in life
from that special person the disciple is following.

I suppose that you could say that I'm a disciple of John Wimber. I've spent a good portion of my life studying John and his
approach to the Christian life. As I said earlier, our church in
Evanston, Illinois, first became familiar with Wimber and the
Vineyard in the early 1980s. My first contact with him came
through a set of cassette tapes my pastor and good friend, Bill
Hanawalt, had ordered from Vineyard Ministries in California.

These three or four cassette tapes contained worship music
that had been recorded at Sunday night church services at John's
Vineyard church in Yorba Linda. As I listened to this music, a
strange thing began happening to me. I began to cry. Keep in

mind that I am, generally, not a crier. Tears don't come easily for me, but when I listened to these intimate love songs being sung to Jesus, my eyelids just couldn't contain the moisture that was gathering inside. I cried my eyes out!

As a musician who loves to compose and arrange, I've trained myself to listen carefully to the unique sounds coming from within a piece of music. In this case, when I was listening intently to the worship music coming out of those Vineyard cassette tapes, the most impressive sound that caused my tears to flow came from a warm electronic keyboard combined with an equally warm, rich tenor voice singing love songs to Jesus. As it turned out later, I found out that this keyboard player with the warm, inviting voice was John Wimber.

To be honest, I was hooked after that.

Within a few months of first listening to these Vineyard worship music tapes, I attended my first "official" Vineyard leadership conference, seeing and hearing John Wimber for the first time. That conference, in the spring of 1985 in Columbus, Ohio, led to many, many more and, as they say in show business, the rest is history.

Now, over the years, well-meaning folks have come up to me, saying, "Marty, be careful. Don't idolize a man. Remember. You're a disciple of Jesus. Not John Wimber." My response to these nice folks who are looking out for me is this. I followed John and his teachings for one reason. Because, as I see it, John Wimber was a man who had been around Jesus. And quite honestly, I can't say that about many pastors I've met over the years.

Oh sure, there are well-meaning leaders who refer to Jesus in their teachings and point to Christ with their ministries, but in John's case, I always sensed that he was one who wasn't all that interested in building himself a ministry, or gathering people into his crowd. In many ways, John seemed to be kind of like those disciples in the New Testament who were never really interested in themselves, but primarily interested in Jesus.

And so, here I am, nearly thirty years after the first time I heard John Wimber singing his heart out to the Master, and all I can say is thanks, John. I needed that. Thanks for being one of those unique guys who always seemed to be interested in hanging around Jesus. Thanks for being a man who didn't promote himself, but always seemed to be promoting Jesus. Thanks John for modeling a lifestyle in Christ that was naturally supernatural, where everyone could play, regardless of their educational background, their social status, their age, sex, or color. Thanks John for spending time with Jesus and then teaching us that "being with the Master" was and still is the highest priority in life and ministry.

As I see it, you did one great job of getting it right. And I, for one, thank you for it.

PRAYER

Jesus, thank you for having men and women in leadership who know that their highest calling in life and ministry is to be with you. Empower me, Holy Spirit, to be a man who, like John Wimber, knows full well the priority of "being with the Master." For your name's sake. Amen!

QUESTIONS FOR YOU TO PONDER

When they saw the courage of Peter and John and realized that they were unschooled, ordinary men, they were astonished and they took note that these men had been with Jesus. (Acts 4: 13)

- If I were put in a similar situation (standing in front of the Sanhedrin), would those in authority see in me what they saw in these two disciples?
- How have I allowed other ministry qualifiers to become higher priorities over simply being one who spends time being with Jesus?

So what is God speaking to you today as you ponder the *Wisdom of Wimber?*

The crux of Paul's advice to Timothy is found in 2 Tim. 4:2-5. "Preach the Word, be prepared in season and out of season;…" (2 Tim 4:2a) Here Paul urges Timothy to be ready to preach the gospel and minister "in season and out of season." The gospel ministry, unlike fresh strawberries, is never out of season. We must be ready and willing to share the life and works of Jesus at any time – when we "feel anointed"…. when we don't "feel anointed," when we have energy and when we don't.

This willingness to minister any time takes self-discipline – an unpopular lifestyle for many of us. We don't mind ministry when we feel like it, but, ministry anytime? That would cramp our style. Yet as Hebrews 12: 6-7 reminds us, children of God who are not disciplined, live as if they have no father. We need to be under the rulership of our Father. When opportunities to minister come our way — it pleased our Father for us to minister. Ministry knows no season.[13]

Eugene Peterson, who pastored the same church for thirty years, wrote a book entitled: it *A Long Obedience in the Same Direction.*[14]

John Wimber, who pastored the same church for twenty years before dying an untimely death, called it "Doin' the Stuff" in season and out.

Jesus of Nazareth, who labored in ministry for three years before being cruelly crucified by those he was ministering to, called it "Taking Up Your Cross."

Let's face it. It's fairly easy to get up in front of a church and do a nice three-point sermon that ends with a snappy take-home Scripture. Once or twice.

But do that same thing fifty plus times per year over a period of several years in the same church, and it starts to get a bit weary. As Wimber says it, it's pretty easy to pick strawberries during strawberry season. But trying to pick a few choice berries in the middle of winter is not fun stuff, is it?

So it is for many pastors across the fruited plain of America. All alone. Underpaid. Overworked. No retirement plan. No pension fund. Just God and a handful of a few faithful friends who are praying God's best for you.

Hmm. Sound familiar, dear pastor?

At times, it feels pretty lonely out there, doesn't it? Pretty scary stuff. I've talked with numerous pastors of smaller churches over the years. Faithful men and women of God, serving Christ in churches where there are no other staff members besides me, myself, and I.

But then…there's Jesus.

The one who has promised to be with us, through thick or thin, supporting our efforts to faithfully preach God's Word, in season and out.

Thanks to the Apostle Paul who wrote his words of encouragement to Timothy, the lonely pastor who was questioning his call, debating about calling it quits. Just think of it. A young man, a disciple of Paul, left (or should I say abandoned) by his mentor to pastor a group of people who didn't think that he was either old enough or wise enough to lead the flock. One lonely pastor, left to do his very best to shepherd a congregation who knew more about quarreling with each other than they did living graciously, in the Spirit, as a loving community of Christ.

But then, there's Jesus.

Wimber served as a prime example to many as a man who simply loved Jesus and then did his very best to love the church he was called to serve. He was a churchman at heart, a gentleman who always loved the church, regardless of how much the church ever loved him back. A man who believed that the highest calling in life was to sell our pearls of great price, so that we could have the honor of serving the Master, feeding his sheep and loving "the hell" out of the flock.

So my fellow pastors: Don't quit. Keep going. You are not

alone. You are not a failure. The Master sees your labor and knows the difficulty of the task. Like Paul reminds Timothy, "Preach the word; be prepared in season and out of season; correct, rebuke and encourage—with great patience and careful instruction" (2 Tim. 4.2). If I understand Jesus correctly, I believe that he said that he will never leave us or forsake us. And if I understand the Bible correctly, it says that, in the end, the good guys will win!

So today, let's keep our eyes on the prize and keep on keepin' on with the Master. For his name's sake.

PRAYER

Jesus, thank you for your faithfulness in your assigned task and thank you for giving us prime examples of men and women who have gone before us, not forsaking their call just because things got hard or because people started to complain. Holy Spirit, indwell and empower pastors today to keep on keepin' on. Give us your strength for us to complete our assignments. For your name's sake. Amen!

QUESTIONS FOR YOU TO PONDER

- How have I pulled back from "preaching God's Word both in season and out"?
- Am I compromising truth?
- Am I pulling back from the full message of the gospel?
- Am I watering down any aspect of Jesus just because things are hard?
- How can I reach out to another pastor today, encouraging him or her to not quit or compromise as he/she strives to finish the good work Jesus has set before them?

So, what is God speaking to you today as you ponder the *Wisdom of Wimber?*

For the time will come when men will not put up with sound doctrine. Instead, to suit their own desires, they will gather around them a great number of teachers to say what their itching ears want to hear. They will turn their ears away from the truth and turn aside to myths." (2 Tim. 4:3-4).

Paul warns Timothy about one of the most distressing realities of being a Christian leader. No matter how faithful and true one is to preaching and ministering the gospel, there are times when some people will turn their ears and hearts away from the truth and will follow teachers and prophets not sent by God. In order to suit their own desires, they would rather hear fables than facts.

Sadly, there are people in the church who grow weary of the "same old gospel." They are unwilling to listen to a message of repentance from sin. Therefore, they seek a clever new message. They seek to be entertained or stimulated or have their egos lifted up.

We need to guard our hearts and ears from this dangerous condition. As good stewards of what we listen to, we should realize this: Not everything preached from the Word is OF the Word![15]

After many years of pastoring in one church, on occasion a well-meaning person will come up to me and politely comment on how I'm constantly preaching about the kingdom of God. I've come to learn over the years that this line usually is code language for "Hey pastor, I'm really getting tired of your sermons!"

In most cases like this, I usually flash my goofy smile and say something nice like: "You're right. I *am* a pretty boring preacher, aren't I?" So the next Sunday, I bring a new joke or a new story, but then go right back to my familiar theme of teaching and preaching on the kingdom message of Jesus.

And yes, people do leave. After numerous years in one church, I guess it's inevitable that folks will grow tired of me and kingdom messages. As I see it, I'm doing pretty well. I've been preaching on the kingdom now for nearly thirty years and counting. Jesus got crucified for doing that after only *three*!

But seriously, I do know, in my heart, that John Wimber was right when he warned pastors that there will be times when God's Word will simply not be enough for some of our impatient parishioners.

But, don't get me wrong.

I've worked hard over the years to improve my preaching and teaching skills and as a pastoral coach; I encourage other pastors to do the same. I'm always looking for creative new ways to tell the same old gospel message, and I know, for a fact, that I've improved a lot since my first sermons I gave back in the mid-1980s.

But here's the rub. Regardless of the many ways we want to spin it, people in our society have glaringly short attention spans and society teaches us to want something new in our lives on a moment-by-moment basis. Madison Avenue learned a long time ago that the American public grows tired and weary very easily, especially when we are presented with the same message regularly. So itchy ears and impatient eyes have become the motivators behind nearly everything we say and do in our culture today.

Hmm. Did God see this coming, or not?

So what's the cure?

On one hand, while I'm fully supportive of doing everything we can to keep our messages life giving, I'm growing more and more suspicious of our seeker-sensitive mentality in American church life. Do you know the kind I'm talking about? It's that push we see in so many churches to feed the need of the consumer, working really hard to entertain our parishioners versus fulfilling our Jesus-given commission to make real disciples.

As Wimber states it, pastors are called to be good stewards of a gospel message that isn't always good news to people who are looking to be entertained.

On the other hand, I believe being a good steward of God's Word also means asking him for both wisdom and power in bringing the good news of Jesus to twenty-first century listeners with three minute attention spans. In a society where instant communication is the tool of choice, I believe the Holy Spirit can and will empower a generation of kingdom-loving, kingdom-believing pastors to find creative and productive ways to love "the hell" out of people, while still bringing the ancient truths of Jesus of Nazareth into this modernized world.

May God be with us all as we do our very best to preach Jesus in a world where Twitter, Facebook, and other forms of social networking are king and queen of the day.

PRAYER

God, changing times are nothing new to you. Your message is ancient but you've always been faithful in helping your servants to bring your Word in digestible packages for each generation in which your people live. Father, while many may be growing tired and weary of your holy Word, help me to keep it fresh and alive in my heart so that my life reflects that freshness to others. For your name's sake. Amen!

QUESTIONS FOR YOU TO PONDER

- Am I bored with the same old-same old of religion?
- If so, what can I do in bringing more of Jesus' eternal life into me so that I won't grow weary in my attempts to bring God's Word to a generation that seemingly has become bored with God and tired of the tried and true gospel message?
- Am I trying to entertain my listeners out of my own strength or am I truly pushing into the presence of God, allowing his goodness to flow from my life into those I hope to serve?

So what is God speaking to you today as you ponder the *Wisdom of Wimber?*

> To continue to listen is essential because Jesus is still Owner-Operator of the church. It is, after all, his ministry, his authority, not ours. Our job is to cooperate. It is the Lord who adds to the church - not men - and he graciously stoops to use our clumsy efforts (Acts 2:47). Church growth theory and practices, though helpful, only tell us where to prune, what fertilizer to use. In no way do they cause or even explain the miracle of conversion growth.[16]

The truth is that John Wimber, who was the founding pastor of the Vineyard movement, was much more than just a church growth specialist. As I see it, he was, first and foremost, a radically obedient servant to Jesus of Nazareth. For John, church growth principles, were simply tools that pastors could use in removing obstacles to growth. As John's quote here so clearly points out, *only* Jesus can cause his church to grow. And quite honestly, I believe that John never expected pastors in the Vineyard to become so obsessed with church growth that we lose our primary focus on becoming faith communities that place Jesus and his kingdom ministry at the center, rather than programs and ministries designed to focus exclusively on numerical growth.

Case in point?

Recently, I talked with a pastor friend of mine who had just returned from a regional pastor's conference. We'll call him Bill to protect the innocent! The leader of the conference (a very good man who happens to pastor a very large, successful church in the area) closed the meetings by asking all of the pastors in the room to dream with him. He asked, "What dream do you have for your church?" After a few moments of prayer and reflection, the leader encouraged each pastor to huddle up with at least one other pastor in the room before leaving, asking them to join, one-on-one, to hear each other's dreams for their churches and then pray for one another before hitting the door.

Bill, our pastor friend, who has struggled over the years with the typical ins-and-outs of shepherding a smaller church, found the suggestion of dreaming a bit intimidating at first. To be honest, for most pastors of smaller churches, it's hard to dream with God after numerous years of serving in churches where attendance and offerings go up and down like a yo-yo. But pray, he did.

By the time Bill looked up to find a fellow-pastor, everyone was already paired up. The only guy available was the leader of the conference. Our friend felt a bit sheepish stepping up to this pastor, knowing that his church is a multi-site, several-thousand-member church. Bill's church has struggled to break the 200 barrier over the years and at the time of this meeting; his church attendance was running well below 100.

Bill took a deep gulp and stepped up to the successful pastor. "My dream," Bill said, "is to make my church into a training center, raising up leaders for the cause of Christ." Without any hesitation, the leader of the conference smiled, and knowing our friend's church very well, he said, "Bill, that's a great dream. But let's get your church over the 200 barrier first and then we can talk training center."

Bill walked away from that conference frustrated. When I heard his story, I was mad. Really mad! Maybe this story affects you that way as well.

As I see it, it's this kind of approach to pastoral ministry, where mission takes a back seat to numbers, which is producing a generation of 3-B pastors.

What is a 3-B pastor, you ask?

A 3-B pastor is any minister or church leader who is addicted to measuring his or her "success" (or failure) in ministry using three major components, utilized in many of our churches, large and small, across North America. I call this triad of components, the 3-Bs: (B)uildings, (B)ucks, and (B)utts in the seats.

If a church is doing well in all of these 3-Bs, hallelujah! God is good and so are we! But pity the poor pastor, ministry overseer, or church, for that matter, who is struggling in any or all of these 3-B numbers! Sadly, in the eyes of much of the Westernized church, if your church meets in a smaller, under-equipped facility, takes in less than $15 to $20 per person on any given Sunday morning, and/or has less than 200 butts in the seats on any given weekend, you're in deep doo-doo, just as my friend Bill found himself on that fateful day at a recent pastor's conference.

John's quote above is a great reminder that it's time for me, and other pastors across North America, to stop our church-growth-at-all-cost madness and return ourselves to becoming churches that measure success by using Jesus' standards, rather than those that are built on principles that, quite honestly, are torn from the pages of successful corporate models of great business practices across the good ole USA.

Jesus, as Wimber states, is still the "owner-operator" of the churches we pastor. What do you say that we move out of the executive chair in our boardrooms, allowing Jesus to be, once again, the President and CEO? In the meantime, you and I, as pastors and ministry workers, can get back to being simple, humble servants of the Master, following his plans for ministry success, not ours!

PRAYER

Father God, I quickly confess that the 3-Bs, where the size of (B)uildings, the total of (B)ucks in the offering, and the number of (B)utts in the seats have consumed me as a pastor. I choose to lay down those church-growth measurement tools so that you can show me once again how you measure success in the church that bears your name. For your name's sake. Amen!

QUESTIONS FOR YOU TO PONDER

- Am I truly seeking the manifest presence of Jesus in my church over and above the pursuit of success with the 3-Bs?
- What might it look like for me to lay down some of the popular church growth principles long enough to focus on greater kingdom purposes, like the care of souls, the

making of disciples, the equipping of the saints, loving "the hell" out of our communities, and practicing the on-going presence of God?

So, what is God speaking to you today as you ponder the *Wisdom of Wimber?*

Church growth theory and practices, though helpful,

only tell us where to prune, what fertilizer to use.

THE WISDOM OF WIMBER
AS I SEE IT

ON WORSHIP

...worship is the act of freely giving love to God.

Probably the most significant lesson that (we) and the early Vineyard Fellowship learned was that worship is the act of freely giving love to God. Indeed, in Psalm 18:1 we read, *"I love you, O Lord, my strength."* Worship is also an expression of awe, submission, and respect toward God (see Ps 95:1-2; 96:1-3).

Our heart's desire should be to worship God; we have been designed by God for this purpose. If we don't worship God, we'll worship something or someone else.[17]

John and Carol Wimber, in their mutual ministry, restored many kingdom truths back to the church of Jesus Christ. God-truths that had been covered over with dust for many years, ancient gems that, when dusted off and practiced anew, renewed God's people back into Jesus-centered, Spirit-empowered lives.

Was Wimber a saintly prophet sent by God? No, not really. He was quick to remind people that he was just a fat man from Missouri doing his very best to get to heaven.

Was he perfect? Far from it. In fact, from all I've read, he seemed a bit remorseful near the end of his life over times when he missed it, going one way when he might have gone another.

But, with that being said, John and Carol Wimber, while not saints, were reformers. And like other reformers who went before them, John and Carol will be remembered as devoted followers of Christ who were willing to color outside the lines of Christian tradition, especially when their artwork would assist the average man or woman sitting in the pew in finding help in getting closer to Jesus!

Probably one of the finest gems that these reformers offered the larger body of Christ was the restoration of intimate worship, or as John says it here..."the act of freely giving love to God."

A careful read of John and Carol's story reveals that this discovery of the fine art of singing intimate love songs to Jesus as a part of worship happened nearly by accident. At this point, it might be good to share with you Carol Wimber's own colorful description of what happened back in the earliest days of the Vineyard.

We began worship with nothing but a sense of calling from the Lord to a deeper relationship with him. Before we started meeting in a small home church setting in 1977, the Holy Spirit had been working in my heart, creating a tremendous hunger for God. One day as I was praying, the word "worship" appeared in my mind like a newspaper headline. I had never thought much about that word before. As an evangelical Christian, I had always assumed the entire Sunday morning gathering was "worship" - and, in a sense, I was correct. But in a different sense there were particular elements of the service that were especially devoted to worship and not to teaching, announcements, musical presentations, and all the other activities that are part of a typical Sunday morning gathering. I had to admit that I wasn't sure which part of the service was supposed to be worship.

After we started to meet in our home gathering, I noticed times during the meeting - usually when we sang - in which I experienced God deeply. We sang many songs, but mostly songs about worship or testimonies from one Christian to another. But occasionally we sang a song personally and intimately to Jesus, with lyrics like "Jesus, I love you." Those types of songs both stirred and fed the hunger for God within me.

About this time I began asking our music leader why some songs seemed to spark something in us and others didn't. As we talked about worship, we realized that often we would sing about worship yet we never actually worshipped - except when we accidentally stumbled onto intimate songs like "I love you, Lord," and "I lift my voice." Thus we began to see a difference between songs about Jesus and songs to Jesus.

Now, during this season when we were stumbling around

corporately in worship, many of us were also worshipping at home alone. During these solitary times we were not necessarily singing, but we were bowing down, kneeling, lifting hands, and praying spontaneously in the Spirit - sometimes with spoken prayers, sometimes with non-verbalized prayers, and even prayers without words at all. We noticed that as our individual worship life deepened, when we came together there was a greater hunger toward God. So we learned that what happens when we are alone with the Lord determines how intimate and deep the worship will be when we come together.

About that time we realized our worship blessed God, that it was for God alone and not just a vehicle of preparation for the pastor's sermon. This was an exciting revelation. After learning about the central place of worship in our meetings, there were many instances in which all we did was worship God for an hour or two.

At this time we also discovered that singing was not the only way to worship God. Because the word worship means literally to bow down, it is important that our bodies are involved in what our spirits are saying. In scripture this is accomplished through bowing heads, lifting hands, kneeling, and even lying prostrate before God.

A result of our worshiping and blessing God is being blessed by him. We don't worship God in order to get blessed, but we are blessed as we worship him. He visits his people with manifestations of the Holy Spirit.

Thus worship has a two-fold aspect: communication with God through the basic means of singing and praying, and communication from God through teaching and preaching the word, prophecy, exhortation, etc. We lift him up and exalt him, and as a result are drawn into his presence where he speaks to us.[18]

Over the next five sections, we will unpack a bit more detail on all the Wimbers eventually learned and taught us about practicing the fine art of worship: the act of freely giving love to God. I hope you'll join us.

PRAYER

Father God, I thank you for the experiences in worship you

gave the Wimbers in those earliest days of the Vineyard. I, for one, was radically transformed as I learned this fine art of freely giving love back to you. Now, all these years later, I'm so thankful that this gift of intimate worship has been restored to your church, but now I say, Abba Father, teach us more! For your name's sake. Amen!

QUESTIONS FOR YOU TO PONDER

- Am I allowing myself and others around me to have the freedom we all need to freely express our intimate worship to God?
- Carol Wimber speaks of not only singing intimate love songs to Jesus, but also the use of bodily expressions in worship such as bowing down, bowing our heads, lifting our hands, kneeling, or even lying prostrate before God. Are these acts of worship "permissible" in my church as acts of worship or do our "traditions" say that well-behaved Christians can't worship in this manner?

So, what is God speaking to you today as you ponder the *Wisdom of Wimber*?

Not only is it helpful to understand why and how we worship God, it is also helpful to understand what happens when we worship God. In the Vineyard we see five basic phases of worship, phases through which leaders attempt to lead the congregation. Understanding these phases is helpful in our experience of God. Keep in mind that as we pass through these phases we are headed toward one goal: intimacy with God. I define intimacy as belonging to or revealing one's deepest nature to another (in this case to God), and it is marked by close association, presence, and contact.

The first phase (of worship) is the *call to worship*, which is a message directed toward the people. It is an invitation to worship. This might be accomplished through a song like, "Come Let us Worship and Bow Down." Or it may be jubilant, such as through the song, "Don't You Know It's Time to Praise the Lord?"

The underlying thought of the call to worship is "Let's do it, let's worship now." Song selection for the call to worship is quite important, for this sets the tone for the gathering and directs people to God. Is it the first night of a conference when many people may be unfamiliar with the songs and with others in attendance? Or is it the last night, after momentum has been building all week? If this is a Sunday morning worship time, has the church been doing the works of God all week? Or has the church been in the doldrums? If the church has been doing well, Sunday worship rides on the crest of a wave. All these thoughts are reflected in the call to worship. The ideal is that each member of the congregation be conscious of these concerns, and pray that the appropriate tone be set in the call to worship.[19]

One of the real benefits from being around a guy like John Wimber was the fact that he not only was a passionate worshipper of God, but he also had an amazing ability to take very holy moments with Jesus and assist others in accessing those powerful experiences as well.

As I see it, it wasn't good enough for John to have a spiritual experience with God by himself or with just a few close friends. John, a pastor who always seemed to be thinking about others, made a career out of finding practical ways the larger body of Christ could access those same holy moments he was experiencing. Thus, the expression that became so popular in the Vineyard: "everybody can play."

Case in point?

John's intriguing list of the five phases of worship. I like to call it five steps in the fine art of worship-making:

1. The Call to Worship.
2. Engagement in Worship.
3. Expressing Our Love.
4. Visitation of God.
5. Generosity Toward God.

Once the folks in the early days of the Vineyard began experiencing God in powerful ways through worship (see our last section where Carol Wimber shares her story), John Wimber set out to help others find their way into God's presence as well. For him, it just wasn't good enough for the Yorba Linda church to be experiencing God in worship. He wanted all of his other pastoral friends in other churches to be experiencing God as well. Thus, he wrote down for us his thoughts on how worship leaders might rearrange their worship times so that it best accomplished our actual goal in worship: positioning God's people in God's loving presence.

So step one, as he called it, is the Call to Worship.

I find it intriguing that so many worship leaders, even today, seem oblivious to the way we do worship in many of our churches. With all the power point graphics, choreographed staging, and multi-colored floodlights, we so often forget that worship is not about entertainment, but coming into the presence of God.

And if we'd ever stop long enough to think about it, coming into the presence of God is a holy thing. And since it's a holy moment, pastors and worship leaders might want to consider how we, as God's people, might want to choose more carefully the way we are entering into his presence. Sadly, so many worship leaders just throw out a "get-the-butts-in-the-seats" kind of song for an opener, while never really giving much thought to what this opening song is all about!

What might change in our worship experiences in many of our churches, if we'd spend more time, preparing more carefully in choosing the songs that might best serve our church community in getting ourselves ready to worship the Lord? Songs of invitation. Songs of encouragement. Songs combined with scriptural readings or other visual presentations that actually invite God's people to begin the trek into his presence.

And what about this challenging thought? Why do so many church leaders in contemporary settings today believe that the "worship" of God begins and ends with our music set? Certainly when we are exploring the importance of calling God's people into his presence, we should never be so limited in our perspective that we believe that it's only by music that people can enter into a time of worshipping God.

Think for a moment how we see this pattern in the Scriptures.

The Songs of Ascent (Psalms 120-134) come to mind as scriptural evidence that the ancient psalmists gave great thought to ways that best prepared God's people as they came closer toward their creator/king. And what about Jesus? In the gospels, we don't see the Master pounding out deep spiritual truths with his followers without first being very careful in inviting them to "come, follow me."

Maybe it's time for pastors and worship leaders to get our heads together before each Sunday morning service and ask God how he might want to call his people into worship today?

Hmm. What a concept!

Seeking God on how we might do church versus just doing it out of our own strength. Thanks, John. I needed that!

Prayer

Father God, as I see it, the fine art of worship-making needs to be restored in your church once again. Thank you for John Wimber's thoughts on how your people might best approach such a holy thing as worship. May you teach us once more how to respect the acts of worship, so that each step we take toward you is well-thought-out and done with great honor and respect. For your name's sake. Amen!

Questions for You to Ponder

- How have I allowed the act of worship to become sloppy in my life?
- Have I become so familiar with the standardized approach to corporate worship in the American church that I've lost the fine art of worship-making?
- What needs to change in my approach toward worship in my church so that I'm more aware of the great need for the "call to worship" as we begin our time together?

So, what is God speaking to you today as you ponder the *Wisdom of Wimber*?

The second phase (of worship) is the *engagement*, which is the electrifying dynamic of connection to God and to each other. Expressions of love, adoration, praise, jubilation, intercession, petition - all of the dynamics of prayer are interlocked with worship - come forth from one's heart. In the engagement phase we praise God for who he is through music as well as prayer. An individual may have moments like these in his or her private worship at home, but when the church comes together the manifest presence of God is magnified and multiplied.[20]

To Wimber, who was a musician at heart, it just wasn't good enough to sit in a pew, listen to a piece of worship music, and not engage with it. That's why it was so painful for him to visit a church and find the leadership team using worship as some form of entertainment or as a warm-up for the pastor's sermon.

Thank goodness this doesn't happen everywhere, but during my days working with Promise Keepers, I visited a church where it was customary for the lead pastor to use the worship time to review his sermon notes, making any last-minute changes before stepping up to the podium. When I asked someone about that, the answer was that the senior pastor enjoyed using the presence of God that comes during worship as the perfect time to get his final thoughts together on what God wanted him to share. Now, at first glance, that sounded like a reasonable answer, but then I remembered what Wimber used to say about engagement in worship:

Engagement = the electrifying dynamic of connection to God and to each other.

Let's be gut-honest here. Worship is not a tool to get us somewhere. Worship is not a mechanism to get God to do something for us. Nor should worship be used as an avenue of entertainment, designed to woo a crowd!

As I see it, worship is for and about God. And not us. Period! It's his time, not ours. So when it's time to worship, isn't it our responsibility as followers of Jesus to forget about ourselves, our egos, our stuff, and engage with him?

I kind of think that Wimber got this engagement in worship thing primarily because he was a musician at heart. Musicians, you see, believe that music, along with all of the creative arts, begs us to be engaged. And when it's worship music, how much more are we called to stop what we're doing, yield our wills and minds to him, and jump feet first into the presence of God?

No spectators please! Just willing participants ready to engage with the Holy God of the Universe.

Oh yeah, I know. The excuses abound. I use 'em at times myself...

- "I just don't like the song the band is playing."
- "I just can't get myself into it today."
- "The worship leader is singing a bit flat."
- "My mind is caught up in my countless troubles."
- "I just had an argument with my spouse on the way to church."
- "Blah. Blah. Blah."

Countless reasons to not engage, but only one reason we must: he's God. We're not!

Louis Armstrong was a great jazz musician. One night, while visiting New York City, some of Armstrong's friends decided to take him to the opera. Being a black jazz trumpeter from New Orleans, opera was not something Armstrong had been exposed too much over the years. After the first act, one of his friends asked him what he thought of the opera thus far. He leaned back in his seat, rolled his eyes, and said, "Well, I'll tell ya, my friend... opera is not my thing, but lookin' at those musicians on the stage and seein' how much they're enjoyin' it, I just gotta believe that just because I ain't receivin', don't mean those cats ain't sendin'!"

As I see it, worship is going on night-and-day in God's presence. For him, there are no commercial breaks, bathroom breaks, or breaks at all. Worship is happening 24-7, 365, forever and ever, amen. The only question that we are faced with is whether or not you and I will actively choose to engage with that worship, or will we allow lesser things to pull us away?

So the next time you or I find ourselves sitting in a church service or small group and someone is up there on the stage doing their very best to lead you and me into worship, I suggest that we do like Louie Armstrong. Go right back into the second act, choosing intentionally to engage with Jesus, the lover of our souls!

PRAYER

Father, my prayer is that I will never be so cold-hearted or flat-footed that I fail to answer the call to fully engage: mind, soul, spirit, and body into worship the very next opportunity I get! You are worthy of my praise whether I feel like worshipping or not. Holy Spirit, give me the precious gift of holy engagement in worship. For your name's sake. Amen!

QUESTIONS FOR YOU TO PONDER

- How have I become dull or disinterested when it comes to corporate worship?
- Have I allowed an 'oh-hum' attitude to overtake me or, worse yet, do I use worship for other purposes? If so, what needs to change on my inside so that I can restore my intentional acts of engagement in worship?

So, what is God speaking to you today as you ponder the *Wisdom of Wimber*?

As we move further in the engagement phase (of worship), we move more and more into loving and intimate language. Being in God's presence excites our hearts and minds and we want to praise him for the deeds he has done, for how he has moved in history, for his character and attributes. Jubilation is that heart swell within us in which we want to exalt him. The heart of worship is to be united with our Creator and with the church universal and historic. Remember, worship is going on all the time in heaven, and when we worship we are joining that which is already happening, what has been called the communion of saints. Thus there is a powerful corporate dynamic.

Often this intimacy causes us to meditate, even as we are singing, on our relationship with the Lord. Sometimes we recall vows we have made before our God. God might call to our mind disharmony or failure in our life, thus confession of sin is involved. Tears may flow as we see our disharmony but his harmony; our limitations but his unlimited possibilities. This phase in which we have been awakened to his presence is called *expression*.

Physical and emotional expression in worship can result in dance and body movement. This is an appropriate response to God if the church is on that crest. It is inappropriate if it is whipped up or if the focal point is on the dance rather than on true jubilation in the Lord.[21]

Back in the day, John and Carol Wimber shepherded a small group of people who had come to the end of themselves. Many had been involved in church life for years, serving diligently, giving their very best efforts to keep the church they attended alive and well. Over time, their energies waned. Business-as-usual had become the status quo. The vibrant church life they had once known and enjoyed had grown into a dry, stale routine.

Hungry for God but tired in body, mind and spirit, this group of worn-out Christ-followers decided to lay down their ministries and simply spend time sitting in God's presence, waiting on him to come to them rather than continuing to work hard at doing church for God.

Over time, during their seasons of waiting on God, the Holy Spirit began teaching these burned-out, dry-as-a-cracker Christians a pattern of corporate worship that brought them new life. Over the years, as God began blessing their broken and worn-out lives with his presence once more, John and Carol began to note a pattern to their worship experiences. This pattern of worship, when practiced faithfully by men and women who truly wanted God's presence more than a typical church experience, became what John eventually called the five phases of worship.

As we've discussed thus far in this section of our book, the first step in the fine art of worship-making is the simple call to worship, followed, second, by our intentional engagement with God in worship. The third phase is where you and I intentionally choose to abandon ourselves and our fleshly interests, allowing ourselves and others to freely express our feelings toward God, which is, quite honestly, a place most Christians in our culture rarely allow ourselves to go.

As I see it, most human beings are conditioned by society on what behavior is appropriate in public and what is not. For example, most Christians grow up in church environments where the word *worship* is just another way of defining the typical Sunday morning service we hold in our church buildings. Sadly, so few Christians today realize that the word *worship*, as found in the Scriptures, is actually referring to a bodily expression!

Did you realize, for example, that the first time the word *worship* appears in the Bible (the Hebrew word is *shachah*) is when father Abraham is found trekking up the mountain, responding in obedience to God's outrageous instructions to sacrifice Isaac, his only son, as a love offering to God? It's here in Genesis 22, we find these words:

Some time later God tested Abraham. He said to him, "Abraham!"

"Here I am," he replied.

Then God said, "Take your son, your only son, whom you love—Isaac—and go to the region of Moriah. Sacrifice him there as a burnt offering on a mountain I will show you."

Early the next morning Abraham got up and loaded his donkey. He took with him two of his servants and his son Isaac. When he had cut enough wood for the burnt offering, he set out for the place God had told him about. On the third day Abraham looked up and saw the place in the distance. He said to his servants, "Stay here with the donkey while I and the boy go over there. We will worship and then we will come back to you."

In this passage of Scripture, *worship* is defined, not as a song to be sung toward God, but as an act of extravagant obedience. Here, Abraham has 1) heard God's invitation to worship, 2) engaged himself by actively moving forward on those things God has invited him to, and now 3) is ready to express his love back to God in extreme ways that, quite honestly, go far beyond any of our comfort zones.

Fortunately, in our day and time, God is not asking us to sacrifice any of our children on his holy alter. Praise God, that act of obedience was accomplished, once and for all, by God, himself, when he took that job on by asking his own Son, Jesus of Nazareth, to die for our sins!

But here's the rub.

While God is no longer looking for any earth-dweller to die for our sins, he is still looking for those who love and trust him to physically engage ourselves in acts of extravagant love, which express our hearts of gratification to a Holy God who loves us so much that he sent his own Son to die for us!

So the next time you and I find ourselves in corporate worship, might I suggest that we practice John Wimber's third phase of worship in full, going far beyond our traditional ways of worship; where opening up a songbook and singing a song or two to God is about as radical as it gets?

How about if we actually tried worshipping like the Hebrew word for *worship* calls us to? In Genesis 22, the word *worship* (*shachah*) actually means *to lay prostrate before God*, which could include humbly laying down our fleshly dreams, while expressing our deep, deep love and appreciation for a God who has done so much to restore us back into right relationship with himself! Let's remember that "Worship is human response to a gracious God, and it needs to be placed in this context if it is to be properly understood."[22]

Hmm.

Now that kind of *worship*, when expressed on Sunday mornings, might look a bit different than most of us are used to, don't you think? But hold on to your hats, folks. Wait till you see what Wimber expected phases four and five of our corporate worship to look like.

PRAYER

God, I confess that my expression of worship seems pretty lame when compared to the *worship* of father Abraham found in Genesis 22. For him, expressing his love to you was, indeed, a costly investment! I am thankful that you are no longer looking for that act of radical obedience, but I do believe that now Jesus has accomplished that sacrificial act of worship on my behalf, I can certainly go a lot further in my expression of love to you, my saving grace. For your name's sake. Amen!

QUESTIONS FOR YOU TO PONDER

- How have I allowed my worship of God to be tamed down because of my fears of what others might say or what the established church might call extreme?
- Am I truly "worshipping," expressing my love freely to my

God, or am I holding back, trying to stay in comfort zones that have been determined by others as appropriate?

So, what is God speaking to you today as you ponder the *Wisdom of Wimber?*

Expression (in worship) then moves to a zenith, a climatic point, not unlike physical lovemaking (doesn't Solomon use the same analogy in the Song of Songs?). We have expressed what is in our hearts and minds and bodies, and now it is time to wait for God to respond. Stop talking and wait for him to speak, to move. I call this, the fourth phase, *visitation*: The almighty God visits his people.

His visitation is a byproduct of worship. We don't worship in order to gain his presence. He is worthy to be worshiped whether or not he visits us. But God "dwells in the praises of his people." So we should always come to worship prepared for an audience with the King. And we should expect the Spirit of God to work among us. He moves in different ways - sometimes for salvation, sometimes for deliverances, sometimes for sanctification or healings. God also visits us through the prophetic gifts.[23]

In all honesty, most Christians are not nearly patient enough, nor are we informed enough to allow God enough time for this phase of worship to happen. In most church settings, we come into worship, sing a few songs to God, and then move right on into the next part of our service, i.e., the announcements, the pastor's message, the offering, etc.

Now don't get me wrong. All of these other activities are vitally important in the life of a vibrant church community, but sadly, most churches today fail to realize that God actually wants to join our worship experience; giving his response to the worship we've been giving him. If a group of Jesus-followers, for example, 1) respond to the call to worship; 2) actively engage with God through acts of worship, and 3) pour out their expressed love toward God, Wimber felt that we should always make room for this fourth phase of worship where we give the stage back to God, allowing him to respond to all he has received from us. But let's face it folks. Most church services across North America today tend to treat our worship times as one-way communication tools, where we dump our worship at the feet of God, but then leave the room before giving him an equal opportunity to respond!

In the earliest days of the Vineyard, it was very customary for God's people to wait in God's presence at the end of our musical worship time, giving the Holy Spirit plenty of opportunity to bring a response to our worship.

But let's be gut honest here.

In truth, the idea of any open space in a Sunday morning gathering is as frightening as hell to much of our Americanized, git-r-done, seeker-sensitive modes of worship. Heaven forbid if we pastors or leaders would actually burn fifteen minutes off the clock, waiting for ole God to respond to our praise! For so many of us, just five minutes of quiet, in the midst of a Sunday morning service, seems like an eternity! And what about the idea of an open mike on the floor where folks in the pews can share a word of encouragement to others after a time of worship? Yikes! To most pastors today, that's an instant recipe for disaster!

So there you have it, my friends.

Phase four of worship can be a beautiful thing: a visitation from God that, quite honestly, can change everything in the life and ministry of our churches. But are we brave enough to actually allow it to happen?

Let me close with this little word of encouragement.

We must keep in mind that all of this stuff in phase four falls under the category of practicing the presence of God. And remember, as Wimber used to say…"Everything down here is all about practice." As I see it, God doesn't expect us to get it right all the time, but he does expect us to practice!

So what if you and I decide at our next corporate worship time to stop ourselves short as we reach the end of phase three in worship? How about as we get to the end of our worship song set, we decide to give five to ten minutes back to God, letting him say or do something if he'd like? Just imagine! God responding, as only he can, with a visitation of his presence!

Hmm.

Sounds kind of scary doesn't it? And, maybe, just maybe, a bit enthralling as well!

Pastor, I dare you to go first!

PRAYER

Heavenly Father, I'm quick to admit that this phase four of worship (a visitation of God) scares me. Turning things over to you looks really good on paper, or in the Bible, but when push comes to shove, Sunday morning is the hardest place to truly allow you to do whatever you want, however you want, and whenever you want! Yet, Holy Spirit, I know the church belongs to you. So with that in mind, I say, come, Holy Spirit, come! Respond to our worship of you, as you wish. For your name's sake. Amen!

QUESTIONS FOR YOU TO PONDER

- What needs to change in my attitude and my actions when it comes to allowing God the freedom to visit his people as he wants instead of how I might desire it to occur?
- Am I in the way of allowing God to respond with his visitation or am I actually brave enough to give him all the space he needs to respond as he chooses?

So, what is God speaking to you today as you ponder the *Wisdom of Wimber?*

The fifth phase of worship is the *giving of substance*. The church knows so little about giving, yet the Bible exhorts us to give to God. It is pathetic to see people preparing for ministry who don't know how to give. That is like an athlete entering a race, yet he doesn't know how to run. If we haven't learned to give money, we haven't learned anything. Ministry is a life of giving. We give our whole life; God should have ownership of everything. Remember, whatever we give God control of he can multiply and bless, not so we can amass goods, but so we can be more involved in his enterprise.

Whatever I need to give, God inevitably first calls me to give it when I don't have any of it - whether it is money, love, hospitality, or information. Whatever God wants to give *through* us he first has to do *to* us. We are the first partakers of the fruit. But we are not to eat the seed, we are to sow it, to give it away. The underlying premise is that whatever we are is multiplied, for good or for bad. Whatever we have on our tree is what we are going to get in our orchard.[24]

Wimber's *five phases of worship*, or as I now call them, five steps in the fine art of worship-making have helped countless worship leaders around the Vineyard movement to better assist God's people as we gathered together for the explicit purpose of coming into God's presence to worship him.

Wimber believed that as you and I journeyed through these five unique phases of worship: the call to worship; worship engagement; expressing our love; being visited by God; and responding in generosity that we could experience intimacy with God; we were experiencing the highest and most fulfilling calling in life. After thirty years of practicing these five phases of worship with the churches I've pastored, I totally concur.

If you recall, earlier in this book, we shared this quote from John Wimber: "It's not enough to be biblically literate; we must also learn to be biblically obedient!"

As I see it, the fifth phase of worship, where we freely give back to God as he has freely given to us, just might be the most important aspect of the true worship experience from a biblical perspective. You see, anytime we come into God's presence, engaging with the king of the universe, there is always a blessing in doing that. And in the truest essence of Jesus' earthly nature, it's always important to give away freely and generously those blessings he grants us as we dwell in his presence.

Wimber used to say it this way, "We get to give, to get to give."

Those who become passionate worshippers of God in this lifetime become, in fact, the ones who have the most valuable gifts to give away to this broken world around us. Intimacy with the king, you see, bestows upon us his favor, and having his favor behooves us to release that favor we've been given to others who desire it.

Think of it this way.

When you and I find our way into God's presence, we find, in the king's throne room, a great treasure chest full of precious heavenly gifts. This treasure chest contains the most valuable gifts the world has ever known. Not diamonds, gold, and silver, but eternal gifts the Holy Scriptures call fruit and gifts of the Spirit. My personal favorites in this treasure chest are priceless gems called faith, hope, and love.

This overflowing treasure chest in God's presence is hidden from the world, but readily available to those who seek it through the words and works of Jesus Christ of Nazareth. As worshippers of the king, you and I can sit in his presence, and as we dwell there for a period, the Holy Spirit begins to place some of these priceless jewels in our coat pockets. As we leave the presence of God, returning back into our fallen world, God asks one simple thing of us: "Give away freely those gifts I've given you as you've been in my presence." As we do this job faithfully, giving away the precious gifts from heaven, we know that when we run out, all we need to do is make a return trip back into God's presence where there's always an abundance of gifts to once again fill our pockets. There's no need for hoarding, because in God's presence, there's plenty of his treasures to fill our lives and the lives of others around us.

But here's the catch.

The moment we try to store up God's rich treasures for ourselves, hoarding them like misers, the goodness of the Spirit tends to turn sour, spoiling just as the manna did in the wilderness, when God's people tried to secure enough for a rainy day. You see, since you and I can now readily access the throne room of God 24-7, 365 days, it's never necessary to hoard or sock away the good gifts of God.

Thus, step five in the fine art of worship-making is freely and generously giving all God has given us as we've been in his presence. And then as our pockets begin to get empty, just pick yourself up, respond to God's call to worship, and begin the five-step process all over again!

We get to give, to get to give, to get to give....

Well, I think you get the picture, right?

PRAYER

Father God, I choose to actively involve myself in this holy treasure hunt where I actively pursue you and your presence, fill myself with your goodness, go give away all you've given me, and then return to your presence once more to dwell with you again. May I never grow tired of this holy cycle of worshipping you, where getting to give, and getting to give is the sacred pattern of a holy life. For your name's sake. Amen!

QUESTIONS FOR YOU TO PONDER

- Am I skipping or short-changing any of the five phases of worship?

- Am I freely giving away all the goodness God is bestowing into me as I learn the fine art of worship-making?
- Am I hoarding God's treasures or am I one, like Jesus, who freely and generously gives away all the Father gives?

So, what is God speaking to you today as you ponder the *Wisdom of Wimber?*

It is pathetic to see people preparing for ministry

who don't know how to give.

ON GIFTS OF THE SPIRIT

..."full of the Holy Spirit" is synonymous

with possessing mature character.

> But select from among you, brethren, seven men of good reputation, full of the Spirit and of wisdom, whom we may put in charge of this task...and they chose Stephen, a man full of faith and of the Holy Spirit. (Acts 6:3,5)
>
> In our book *Power Points*, Kevin Springer and I tried to clarify the different ways Luke uses the concept of "filling," "filled," and "being full." Luke employs three Greek words for filling, and they all give a slightly different twist to its meaning.
>
> Acts 6:5 describes filling more like a *character quality* or disposition in which a person is habitually controlled by God's Spirit. Stephen was full (*pleres*) of faith and the Holy Spirit (see also Luke 4:1; 11:24). In the Acts 6 passage above, the "full of the Holy Spirit" is synonymous with possessing mature character.[25]

Isn't it sad?

So much of what we see being done by well-meaning Christians now-a-days is not "full of the Spirit," but full of ____ !

Well, you know. Something else. You fill in the blank.

Now, please, don't get me wrong. I've been around the church for thirty plus years. I love the people of God and would not want to be associated with anyone else or hang out anywhere else. I pastor God's people and will always defend the church to the bitter end. But as one who loves the bride of Christ, may I quickly add that it sure seems as though we don't know jack when it comes to being "full of the Spirit."

Wimber had it right back in the day when Kevin Springer and he wrote their classic book called *Power Points*. A man or woman who believes that he or she is "full of the Spirit" must realize that Jesus is looking for so much more from that person than just being a charismatic worker of signs and wonders or a dynamic speaker who woos the masses.

Certainly, one who claims to be "full of the Spirit" will be able to accomplish amazing things in life, because indeed, the power that raised Christ from the dead is now dwelling inside us. But sadly, so many Christians today forget that being "full of the Spirit," as Wimber points out here in the Scriptures, is referring to issues of mature character as much as it is referencing prowess in the Spirit.

I can't tell you how many times I've run into men and women, both Pentecostal and non-Pentecostal, over the years who operate in great power of the Spirit, but absolutely stink when it comes to operating out of the basic fruit and gifts of the Spirit of God: fruit like humility, gentleness, kindness, compassion, and gifts like faith, hope, and love.

As I see it, this is the exact reason Paul had to write his famous love chapter (First Corinthians 13) to the folks "full of the Spirit" in Corinth. Sure, they were going around their city blasting out evil spirits, curing sicknesses, and delivering people from demons. They were proclaiming clearly, the victory of Christ to the lost and bringing salvation to many households. But alas, if I read Paul clearly, his friends in Corinth were doing these powerful things in ways that betrayed the very essence of the Spirit of Christ, which was dwelling within them!

And so Paul, ever so gently, but yet in no uncertain words, warned his brothers and sisters like in First Corinthians 13: 1-3:

> If I speak with human eloquence and angelic ecstasy but don't love, I'm nothing but the creaking of a rusty gate. If I speak God's Word with power, revealing all his mysteries and making everything plain as day, and if I have faith that says to a mountain, "Jump," and it jumps, but I don't love, I'm nothing. If I give everything I own to the poor and even go to the stake to be burned as a martyr, but I don't love, I've gotten nowhere. So, no matter what I say, what I believe, and what I do, I'm bankrupt without love (The Message).

Wimber, as a person who operated in great power with the Holy Spirit, equally reminded us back in the day that to be a man or woman who was truly "full of the Spirit" meant that we needed to address issues of character, making certain that we were operating in gifts of faith, hope, and love as much as the gifts of power. To Wimber, a man of God who went around healing the sick by day, but then went home and was abusive to his wife and kids, was not a man "full of the Spirit." Nor was the preacher who, by the Spirit of God, rants and raves at his congregation about the sinful condition of the church while being one who later went home and secretly viewed porn on his computer.

John used to pray it for himself and others this way: "Father, help us to grow up in the ways of God before we grow old."

Probably not a bad prayer for us "full of the Spirit" folks to be praying here in the twenty-first century? Don't you think?

PRAYER

God, I'm so very sorry that I, for one, can go off "full of the Spirit" and do some pretty amazing things in your name, but then in the same breath, be cold-hearted, hot-tempered, and self-centered, defying the very definition the Scriptures give us on being a man "full of the Spirit." Father, search me and cleanse me inside and out, making my character and integrity "full of the Spirit." For your name's sake. Amen!

QUESTIONS FOR YOU TO PONDER

- How have I focused exclusively on the power of the Spirit while forgetting to pray the life-giving prayer of Wimber… "God, grow me up before I grow old?"
- Is my inner character and integrity "full of the Spirit" or am I just seeking those external power gifts of the Spirit that Paul addressed in his letter to the Corinthians?

So, what is God speaking to you today as you ponder the *Wisdom of Wimber?*

TROPHIES, TALENTS, TRAITS OR TOYS

The gifts of the Spirit have nothing to do with personal ambition or career orientation. They are not given to build individual
reputations, to warrant superior positions in the local church, or
to demonstrate spiritual advancement.

The gifts of the Spirit are not trophies, talents, traits or toys. The
gifts of the Spirit are God's supernatural expressions of love,
caring, kindness, healing and concern - bestowed upon us and
through us.[26]

Sadly, we well-meaning Christians can take the bountiful
blessings of God and turn them, as Wimber states here, into
trophies, talents, traits, or toys. How often, in my lifetime,
have I seen anointed men and women of God run amok, taking
the anointing given to them by God, and using it for self-centered
purposes? All the while, the Lord sits sadly off to the side waiting
for someone to be humble enough to do it the right way: Someone who can be trusted with the blessings of God; Someone who
won't treat the fruit and gifts of the Holy Spirit with such disdain; Someone, like Jesus, who will learn to prefer and defer their
personal wills to the interest of the Father, instead of insisting on
having it their way.

I don't get visions very often in my life. However, back about
twenty years ago when Sandy and I were pastoring our first Vineyard church in Iowa City, we attended a big church leadership
conference being held in our area. It was being hosted by a well-
known pastor at the time and literally hundreds and hundreds of
key leaders from major churches across the Midwest were there
to take in this exciting event. Some big-name pastors were scheduled to speak at this conference and I remember feeling the buzz
in the lobby as the doors opened on that first evening. People ran

to the front row seats, making sure that they would be close to all the action!

Sandy and I found some seats about halfway down toward the front and settled in for the excitement. Worship, of course, preceded the first speaker, and there was an excitement in the air as the lights came down and the event was ready to roll. I recall the worship leader that night working the crowd, picking up on the anticipation we all had for the evening. One rock-em, sock-em praise song after another kept the crowd on their feet, moving to the music. I felt a bit uneasy about the worship session, sensing that it was more like a carnival than a place where we should be meeting with God. I sat down and began to reflect on why I was there and why I had allowed myself to get so caught up in the excitement of the evening. Near the end of the worship set, the band finally changed gears, slowing things down a bit with the old hymn, *Be Thou My Vision*. I closed my eyes, lifted my hands, and sang this song to Jesus with as much passion as I could muster.

Suddenly, in my mind's eye, I was standing in the midst of a great hall filled with people. It was a magnificent banquet hall and folks were dressed to the hilt. Apparently the king had invited all of us to attend a banquet held in the honor of Jesus and the royal palace was a-buzz with excitement. As the crowd filed its way into the large banquet room, I took note of a long line of tables lined up along both sides of the hall. The tables were decorated nicely with placards above each one. It had the feel of a tradeshow, where booths are set up for vendors to display their wares, but in this case, the placards above each booth really intrigued me. On one side of the room, all the gifts of the Spirit were listed on the placards. As my eyes scanned the long row of tables, I saw that the first booth said the gift of healing; the next, the gift of tongues; followed by yet another where the gift of wisdom was being distributed. On the opposite side of the room, the signage advertised the fruit of the Spirit. The first booth had faith; the next, hope; followed by the next, love.

People were flocking to the tables. Apparently this banquet was being held by the king to freely distribute his gifts and his fruit to his people. I was excited. I thought to myself, "I better get over to those tables as quickly as I can before they run out of gifts!"

Then it hit me.

As I saw the people flocking to the tables, even getting a bit rowdy, pushing each other to get to the gifts they wanted, I suddenly felt very remorseful. Here I was, one of God's children, pushing and shoving others, trying to outrun them to get the fruit and the gifts I wanted for my life.

In my guilt and shame, I looked up and across the room, there he was. At the front of the great banquet hall, sat the guest of honor. It was Jesus, sitting there all by himself at the head table. He looked very sad. As my eyes caught his, he beckoned me to step away from the busy tables. At first, I was hesitant. I really wanted my share of these fruit and gifts and by going over to Jesus, I would lose my place in line. Finally, after a few more glances at the Master, I decided to tear myself away from the madness and go over to Jesus. As I stepped up to him, he beckoned me to sit down next to him. I could tell that he was very disappointed at the way everyone was acting. I felt his deep sadness and stayed there with him for some time, giving him the undivided attention no one else seemed interested in doing.

After a while, the crowds died down. People had come and gone. The room was a mess. People had grabbed all of the gifts and fruit and walked out of the room, never even coming up to the guest of honor to acknowledge or thank him for the party or for the party favors! Inside, I felt a bit cheated. Since I had stepped out of line earlier in the evening, I missed the opportunity to get my share of gifts. Jesus looked at me and I was aware that he could read my thoughts. Without a word, he stood up, took me by the hand and walked me over to one of the empty tables. The table was marked love. He reached down behind the empty table and pulled out a gift with my name on it. Then, we went to the second table. He did the same thing. Before the evening was done, Jesus had escorted me to many tables, all of which had specially wrapped gifts with my name written on them, all hidden away behind each table!

I looked into his face and knew with certainty that it was Jesus' intent to escort each individual guest to the tables that evening, doing exactly what he had done for me. But sadly, few were patient enough, first and foremost, to go sit with the Master, allowing *him* to choose what fruit and gifts God had especially set aside for us.

I'll never forget that graphic vision of twenty years ago. And I hope by sharing it here with you today, you too, will remember that the gifts and fruit of the Spirit are not ours, but his. And these same gifts are best accessed by, first and foremost, going over to Jesus, sitting with him, and allowing him to take us to his distribution tables. For his name's sake!

PRAYER

Jesus, forgive me when I take the gifts and fruit of the Spirit and treat them as trophies, talents, traits, or toys. Your gifts are sacred to you, Lord, and I, for one, would prefer to dwell in your presence, waiting for you to release your gifts to me, than to take it into my own hands, trying to operate in gifts that, quite honestly, will always belong to you. For your name's sake. Amen!

QUESTIONS FOR YOU TO PONDER

- How might I be misusing the fruit and gifts of the Spirit, unwittingly trying to operate in these gifts out of my own strength instead of deferring to and preferring Jesus' personal invitation to join him as he determines which gifts and fruit might best fit me and the work he has for me to do?
- Am I looking over my shoulder at others and the gifts they have, becoming envious of others while ignoring the gifts Jesus has specifically picked out for me?

So, what is God speaking to you today as you ponder the *Wisdom of Wimber?*

> (When discussing spiritual gifts) Paul does not give the impression that in the Christian life some people are players and others are spectators. Christians are all players. Some of us might prefer to be spectators because it is safer just to watch. Sometimes it can be fun to watch because it is a good chance to criticize others. It is easier to be a spectator than a participant. But Paul does not give us that option. He indicates that everyone is to participate.[27]

For Wimber, it was not good enough to have a church with just a few select leaders operating in the gifts of the Spirit. In fact, he would go to great strides to prove his point that, indeed, everybody can play when it comes to healing the sick, casting out darkness, and caring for the broken-hearted.

I recall the very first Wimber conference I attended in Columbus, Ohio, in the spring of 1985. After about thirty minutes of intimate worship, Wimber sat at his keyboard and taught us about the healing ministry of Jesus. His favorite passage was Luke 4:18-19. He called it Jesus' job description.

> The Spirit of the Lord is on me, because he has anointed me to proclaim good news to the poor. He has sent me to proclaim freedom for the prisoners and recovery of sight for the blind, to set the oppressed free, to proclaim the year of the Lord's favor.

Then, for the next forty minutes or so, Wimber worked his way through the Gospel of Luke and the Book of Acts, showing us numerous examples where Jesus modeled this same job description and then released his friends and comrades to go in his name to do the same. At that point, when most conference leaders who operate in the gifts of the Spirit would heal the sick, speak prophesies over people, and impress the audience with their spiritual prowess, he closed his Bible and began to do just the opposite.

In Columbus that day, as he sat on a stool next to his keyboard he first asked people who wanted prayer for healing to come forward. Then, rather than getting up and praying for these folks, he asked for any children in the audience to come up front with him. I recall a handful of kids bravely came up on the stage, gathering around him. And with the patience of a loving grandpa, he encouraged the children to gather round those who needed prayer and after about five minutes of simple instructions, folks who needed healing were being blessed big time as the powerful presence of the Spirit began moving across the room. Later that day, he asked for those who received healing that morning to come tell their stories and I recall a large number of folks sharing amazing testimonies on how the Lord touched them powerfully as these kids prayed for them.

"You see," Wimber proclaimed, "Everybody can play!"

For years, as he traveled across the USA and Canada, he would often do such things like this in order to teach the church at large that God isn't looking for superstars with great spiritual prowess but simple, everyday folks who will humbly act in obedience to Jesus' transferrable commission to go, pray for the sick, cast out darkness, and love "the hell" out of those who are looking to Jesus for help.

At times, this approach to the spiritual gifts would spark anger from conference goers. I recall one evening in Detroit, when he turned the entire meeting over to one of his associates and went back to his hotel room, leaving thousands of people who came to see the great John Wimber greatly disappointed. My good friend, Pastor Steve Nicholson of Evanston, IL, was a recipient of one of those kinds of evenings with Wimber. As Steve tells his story, he called him up onto the stage, said, "Steve, I don't have anything, do you?" Steve took a deep breath and said to John, "Maybe you could pray for pain in people's backs." Wimber said, "That's a good idea...you take it from here. I'm going back to the hotel...and Steve...welcome to the healing ministry of Jesus!"

Some thought it laziness or carelessness on the part of Wimber to do such things, but in all honesty, it was all strategically calculated to prove his point that when it comes to operating in the gifts of the Holy Spirit, literally everyone can play.

Too bad the church at large has forgotten this important message over the years. I still cringe when I see big-name preachers and healers call attention to themselves behind the podiums of churches across America. Just recently, I was at a meeting where a "great man of God" was talking about the powerful gifts of the Spirit and then he spent the next forty minutes bringing people up so that they could be healed by the laying on of his hands. Meanwhile, we in the audience were left to sit and watch the great healer of God do his work. I sat there that day, remembering my first Wimber conference in Ohio back in 1985. I leaned over to Sandy and whispered, "Gosh, I sure miss John and his amazing, "everybody can play" approach to ministry, don't you?"

PRAYER

Father, I thank you for the amazing truth that the powerful gifts of the Holy Spirit are for everyone. May I always be generous and otherly when it comes to the operation of the gifts of the Spirit and may your entire church work together in utilizing these amazing gifts to bless you and your kingdom. May we all learn to play together and share freely. For your name's sake. Amen!

QUESTIONS FOR YOU TO PONDER

- How has my theology on the gifts of the Spirit been askew?
- Am I acting as though these powerful gifts are reserved for just a few or am I teaching and modeling a lifestyle where these amazing gifts of God can flow through all, at any time and in any place?

So, what is God speaking to you today as you ponder the *Wisdom of Wimber?*

GRACELETS

In 1 Corinthians 12: 8-12, Paul names *some* of the spiritual gifts that God distributes: words of wisdom, words of knowledge, faith, gifts of healing, miraculous powers, prophecy, the ability to distinguish between spirits, tongues and interpretation of tongues. Many of us have been taught that this list refers to a one-time, permanent endowment for each person.

But I believe that Paul is not talking here about a dispensing of permanently held spiritual gifts. He is talking about passing touches of the Spirit at different times in different settings. Russell Spittler of Fuller Seminary calls them "gracelets." I like that name. It implies that these are little expressions of God's grace. They come and they go, like fragrant flowers that open and close. In fact, they can come and go in milliseconds. One time a certain gift goes to one person. At another time it goes to another person. At any given time a person could minister in prophecy, in tongues, in healing, or in some other form of blessing for the good of others. That would be hard to accomplish in a church where most members are expected to be passive observers.

These are delicate nuances in our relationship with God, and we have to be sensitive enough to respond to them. If we do not, we will never learn to move in the power of the Holy Spirit. [28]

I believe that one of the most revolutionary teachings Wimber brought to the table on the subject of spiritual gifts was his belief that the use of the gifts of the Holy Spirit (i.e., operating in the power of the Holy Spirit) was for everyone and that the gifts were not "one-time permanent endowments" that Christians owned, but were "passing touches of the Spirit," available to all.

In the world of Spirit-endowed, Spirit-empowered Christianity, we tend to see many who, sadly, treat the gifts of the Holy Spirit as badges they have earned. Our previous section addresses that unfortunate situation. Sometimes, this concept of private ownership can become so cemented into the charismatic or Pentecostal mindset; we find churches where men and women strut across the stage, believing they are the best thing to happen to the church since Jesus of Nazareth! I recall working with one very nice man who believed that he had been given the gift of healing, but *only* for headaches! This man served as an elder in a church where I worked and when people would ask him for healing prayer, he'd turn them down if their ailments weren't associated with head pain. Maybe once or twice, I did see him step outside his ownership box and pray half-heartedly for someone with the flu!

Let me be frank. As I see it, this ugly concept of owning the gifts of the Spirit, or being given only one gift to use, is repulsive in the sight of God. And it's time to restore some sensibility to the church when it comes to this goofy belief that you and I can control or manipulate the way God wants to utilize his gifts in his church.

Sadly, a good portion of the evangelical church in the twentieth century saw such misuses and misunderstandings of the gifts, and they decided that it's simply better to step away from the table, proclaiming that these power gifts of the Spirit have all died out, so we don't have to worry about them anymore! But, honestly now, isn't that just moving from one extreme to another?

Wimber brought a fresh revelation on the spiritual gifts: A view that helped restore the gifts of the Spirit back to the larger church, while also addressing the great misuses of those same gifts by those who believed them to be theirs to use at their own discretion. In countless settings, Wimber was so excellent in demystifying the gifts of the Spirit while also giving permission for the common man or woman in the pew to believe that they could operate in these gifts as well as the anointed pastor on the stage.

John's concept of gracelets, you see, brought the gifts back to the God who actually owns and operates them. In truth, it is Jesus of Nazareth, the Resurrected Son of God, who actually owns the gifts of the Spirit! And as we learn to follow him, deferring to and preferring his will over ours, Jesus can then work with the Holy Spirit in the use of those gifts as needed. One author described the operation of the gifts of the Spirit in this lifetime as following "the dancing finger of God." I like that.

When I walk through this life, believing proudly that I've been given a gift or two of the Holy Spirit, acting as though the use of those gifts comes from my directive, I'm dangerously close to becoming the owner/operator rather remaining as a simple servant. And if you and I want to follow the commands found in the gospels correctly, Jesus is still looking for humble, obedient servants who will do his will at his discretion, not independent franchisers looking to build a ministry for themselves!

So there you have it, my friends. As Wimber saw it, the power gifts of the Holy Spirit are for today. Case closed. But sadly, from his perspective, the way so many contemporary Christians operate with these gifts does more damage to the kingdom of God than to help it. Thus, Wimber taught us to treat the gifts of the Spirit with tender, gentle care, seeing them as gracelets released by the Spirit on all believers for certain times and certain situations. From this theology, countless men and women who never viewed themselves as professionals were encouraged to believe that Jesus enjoyed releasing his gifts upon us as we simply go out in his name, loving "the hell" out of everyone we meet.

Hmm.

Maybe it's time for the whole church to take a good refresher course on Holy Spirit gracelets once again?

PRAYER

Holy Spirit, I thank you for your gracelets, your gifts that are released at the command of Jesus, and by the power of God. I, for one, want to learn how to operate in all of your gifts, allowing your gracelets to flow through me, as you direct, and at times you desire. May I always be open and willing for your gracelets to flow through me. For your name's sake. Amen!

QUESTIONS FOR YOU TO PONDER

- How have I limited the use of the gifts or, worse yet, treated the beautiful gracelets of the Holy Spirit as personalized gifts to be used in my way, at my discretion, and in my timing?
- What might it look like for me to change my point of view on these gifts of the Spirit and learn the fine art of following "the dancing finger of God" as he releases his gracelets amongst the body of Christ for his kingdom purposes?

So, what is God speaking to you today as you ponder the *Wisdom of Wimber*?

The manifestation of the Spirit is not supposed to be the exception; it is supposed to be the norm. To how many of us does God give spiritual gifts? "To *everyone.*" Someone might think, "Not to me. What Paul is talking about hasn't ever happened to me." My answer is "Yes, it has! You just didn't have the theology, the practice, or the encouragement to recognize it and respond."

Most of us, frankly, are just too dull and lethargic about our Christian witness and responsibility to be able to release the gifts. Furthermore, many of us are ignorant about spiritual gifts simply because we have not received biblical teaching about them and have not seen healthy examples of them (1 Cor. 12: 1). It is part of the job of apostles, prophets, evangelists, pastors and teachers to encourage and prod the church to operate in the gifts.[29]

For Wimber, it wasn't good enough to say that he believed in something. For him, belief always meant doing something about it.

So when it came to spiritual gifts, it wasn't good enough for John to say that he believed in the existence of spiritual gifts. He wanted both a personal life and a church where the spiritual gifts were fully functioning: a church fully aware and fully alive in the gifts of God!

When we read Paul's letter to the Corinthian church (First Corinthians 12 in The Message), we find a very similar attitude.

What I want to talk about now is the various ways God's Spirit gets worked into our lives. This is complex and often misunderstood, but I want you to be informed and knowledgeable....God's various gifts are handed out everywhere; but they all originate in

God's Spirit. God's various ministries are carried out everywhere; but they all originate in God's Spirit. God's various expressions of power are in action everywhere; but God himself is behind it all. Each person is given something to do that shows who God is: Everyone gets in on it, everyone benefits. All kinds of things are handed out by the Spirit, and to all kinds of people! The variety is wonderful:

wise counsel

clear understanding

simple trust

healing the sick

miraculous acts

proclamation

distinguishing between spirits

tongues

interpretation of tongues.

Just imagine what the church of Jesus Christ could look like and the effectiveness we might have in our world today, if more churches were informed, knowledgeable, and operating in these same gifts Paul mentions in his letter to the Corinthian church!

Back in the day, some called a church community who encouraged everyone to operate in the spiritual gifts a church with "body ministry." As I see it, it might be good if that term were restored to the church again today. "Body ministry" meant that on any given Sunday morning, the gathered saints would come expectant; not only to receive from the Lord and from each other, but they would also come believing that the Holy Spirit was gifting them as well to bring encouragement to others during their time together. Certainly that seemed to be Paul's expectation of the gatherings of God's people in Corinth! Look at what he instructed them to do in chapter 14:26:

> So here's what I want you to do. When you gather for worship, each one of you be prepared with something that will be useful for all: Sing a hymn, teach a lesson, tell a story, lead a prayer, provide an insight (The Message).

Today, Sunday morning church services look and feel more like a concert or a lecture hall where all the hard work is being done on the stage. Sadly, in many congregations across America, about ten percent of the Christians are doing the heavy lifting (i.e. teaching, preaching, leading worship, teaching Sunday School, etc. etc.) while ninety percent sit in the comfy pews, sipping gourmet coffee while doodling on their iPhones!

Heaven forbid, pastors and overseers!

John Wimber envisioned a church where the pastors, teachers, prophets, apostles and evangelists (see Ephesians 5) were commissioned by Jesus to equip the saints to do the ministry of the Spirit, not stand up on the stage and show folks how good we are at it! Shame on us for entertaining the troops while Satan traffics our world, oppressing the good citizens of our planet. As I see it, it's time to restore "body ministry" where everybody who calls themselves a follower of Christ is fully trained, equipped, and sent out as commissioned soldiers to love "the hell" out of the world, while operating in the full array of the gifts (and fruit) of the Holy Spirit.

Anybody wanna sign up? Jesus is calling. Will we respond?

PRAYER

Jesus, you've provided your church with everything we need to fulfill your commission to go and love. The powerful gifts of the Holy Spirit are readily available to any and all who might respond to that call. As a pastor, may I step up to my officer's commission and do my job of not only operating in these gifts myself, but spend my days training, equipping, and sending out my brothers and sisters, in the knowledge and power of these Holy Spirit-given gifts as well. For your name's sake. Amen!

QUESTIONS FOR YOU TO PONDER

- How am I choking off Jesus' commission to train, equip, and send out laborers into the harvest field?
- Am I sending folks out with everything the Holy Spirit has given them? Are they trained in the gifts of the Spirit? Are they knowledgeable?

- Are they encouraged to operate in the full array of fruit and gifts of the Spirit? If not, what changes do I need to make in my job as pastor/overseer?

So, what is God speaking to you today as you ponder the *Wisdom of Wimber*?

In time a (spiritual) gift evolves into a ministry. So, regarding hospitality, if they exercise hospitality frequently, they soon have the ministry of hospitality. A ministry may or may not be accompanied by formal recognition from church leadership. But that is not crucial. Why? Because our focus is on service to others.

So it is that there is a *role*, a *gift* and a *ministry*. One can lead to the next, and there is no sharp line of distinction between them.

Like hospitality, intercessory prayer can be a *role*, a *gift* or a *ministry*. Most of us pray for others as a matter of course, as part of our Christian life. But sometimes there is a supernatural unction, an anointing, that comes upon us to pray for someone in particular. That is the *gift* of intercessory prayer. A habitual exercise of that *gift* produces the *ministry* of intercessory prayer.[30]

According to Wimber, all spiritual gifts belong to God, and since Jesus, the Son of God, has commissioned his followers to continue the kingdom ministry that he started, all Christians living in every generation until the time of Jesus' return, have available to them the same array of spiritual gifts we find operating in the first century church. John taught us to stop thinking of spiritual gifts as something the church owns or as tools available only to a few select leaders.

To John, spiritual gifts are gracelets, readily available to all followers of Jesus, and it's our job, as maturing Christians, to use these powerful gifts from the Holy Spirit not as toys or badges to impress others, but as kingdom tools of love, designed to bless and encourage as we go.

Over the years, as some of us began approaching spiritual gifts in this way, a problem began to seemingly arise. If Wimber was right about everybody getting to play, where every Christian has full right to utilize all the gifts of the Spirit, why is it then, that some seem to operate in those gifts in stronger anointings than others? That question was a good one, and it still is.

Wimber addressed this issue very wisely and he would often talk about the differences between a role, a gift, and a ministry. As I see it, it was this explanation that helped many better understand the seemingly different levels at which various Christians operate in spiritual gifts. Let's take healing, for example.

Wimber was emphatic about the fact that he believed Jesus commissions every believer to the ministry of healing. Keep in mind that he believed that healing, as a gift, belonged only to the Holy Spirit and that no one owned or operated that gift except Jesus. So, when Jesus commissions us to his healing ministry, he is actually commissioning all of us to go and love others, praying for the sick along the way. With that commission in mind, our job then is to pray for the sick, and it's God's job to release the gifts of healing as we go.

It was John's personal experience that as he responded in obedience to "go and pray for the sick," he was playing his role as a believing Christian, responding to the commission Jesus gives us. Over the years as he continued in the "role" of obedient follower of Christ, praying for the sick as commanded by the Master, the gifts of healing would often accompany him as he went. Over time, as he literally prayed for hundreds of people, the "gift" seemed to follow him in increased measure. At that point of his life, many would have looked at him and said that he operated in the "gift" of healing. During some seasons of his life, there was such an increased anointing; some would say he had the "ministry" or "office" of healing. All the while, he never changed his viewpoint on what his "role" was (praying for the sick), but he did realize that God was seemingly stepping up his part as he prayed, releasing the "gifts" of healing, and at times, the "ministry" of healing in response to his obedience.

Thus, Wimber explained, while we might see increased anointing on a person, making us think that person has moved from "role" to "gift" to "ministry," in truth, it is simply God pouring out more of the gift as the person becomes more comfortable and experienced in using the gift God is giving.

Think of it this way.

Just as we might see a master musician making amazing melodies come out of a grand piano as compared to the beginning piano student clunking on those same keys, so it is with the use of spiritual gifts. Over time, as we practice our role, working faithfully alongside God's gifts, we learn the fine art of using God's tools in ways that can look and sound very impressive to others.

But here's the truth.

Whether it be a master artist sitting at the keyboard or a nine-year old beginner, the grand piano they are playing on still belongs to the concert hall! When it comes to spiritual gifts, they all still belong to God, and we get the joy of learning to play on instruments made in heaven!

Sorry, gotta go. Time for some more piano lessons! Anybody wanna join me?

PRAYER

Father, thank you for the gifts of the Spirit, which are readily available to all of us. May I faithfully respond to Jesus' commission and play my role, using the gifts, not for my personal gratification, but for your kingdom purposes. May I grow in my interactive experiences with your gifts, becoming more proficient and appreciative of these wonderful tools of the Spirit. For your name's sake. Amen!

QUESTIONS FOR YOU TO PONDER

- So where am I, a novice in my role as one who utilizes the gifts of the Holy Spirit for kingdom purposes?
- Why am I hesitant to sit down at the grand piano? Am I ashamed that my "music" might sound childish? Am I afraid to be seen as a learner?
- What might my life look like if I decided to take a few more lessons in the fine art of spiritual gifts?

So, what is God speaking to you today as you ponder the *Wisdom of Wimber?*

ON COMMUNITY

Koinonia ... means "holding our lives in common,..."

WELCOME TO THE GARDEN

Loving one another is not just another good idea; it is one of Christ's great blessings. Fellowship is the garden in which the fruit of the Spirit multiply, the place in which eternal life is lived out here on earth.[31]

John Wimber was a lot of things to a lot of people: He was a godly man, a preacher, a teacher, a pastor, an evangelist, a worshipping musician, a reformer, a revivalist, and an agent of change.

But deep down inside, as I see it, Wimber was primarily a churchman. He was a man who absolutely loved the church of Jesus Christ and wanted it to be all Jesus envisioned it to be.

For Wimber, the church was much more than a building or an incorporated entity. The church was a community of gathered saints. A vast garden made up of numerous individual plants: plants gathered together by the hands of the master gardener.

I believe that in his mind, any group of gathered saints represented a planting of the Lord. And while he was best known for themes like Power Evangelism and Power Healing, when it was all said and done, I believe that John and Carol Wimber should be remembered for their deep, deep hunger to see the church, the community of gathered saints, be the rich, rich garden Jesus desires it to be.

Let's be honest. Community—true Christian community—is not an easy thing to accomplish in any generation. Deep within the human spirit, you see, is a fleshly drive for independent thinking, self-sufficiency, and self-promotion. And while the freedom to be ourselves is a good, God-given right, there is a deeper truth about us human beings found within the heart of God, our Creator. That truth is spelled out very clearly at the beginning of the Scriptures. In Genesis 2:18 we find God speaking these important words: "It is not good for the man to be alone."

Now, while many take this verse and apply it only to marriage, I believe the deeper truth here is that God knows that a man (or a woman), when left alone for long periods, will eventually become dangerously self-centered, focused exclusively on his or her self's own wants and needs. Thus, in God's great wisdom, our Creator put within all human DNA an unction in our soul to live together in community. And while our drive for independence, so many times, wins out, history proves that the very best of humankind shines when we choose to live together with others, sharing our individual lives with our fellow human beings.

The best gardens, you see, are made up of a wide variety of plants. Oh sure, 1,000 acres of potatoes, corn, or soybeans produces food for the masses, but in God's economy, a real garden is one that offers not only a rich variety of fruits and vegetables, but also flowering plants that produce pleasing offerings to the eyes and the nose as well! In God's economy, a rich garden is not only a place to feed your stomach, but a quiet place to feed your spirit as well.

So, it is with the community of saints. When you and I can lay down our self-centeredness and our self-consumption long enough to let true community happen, the overall effect in our lives is absolutely amazing. Gosh, to be honest, you might even be tempted to call it Power Community! And this is why John and Carol Wimber spent so much time as churchmen, encouraging the beautiful expression of Christian community in a generation where self-centered "all-about-me" thinking so often prevails.

Over the next few sessions let's take a stroll and explore the beauty of Christian community. Take your time, now, there's so much to experience in the garden of the Lord!

PRAYER

I must admit, Father, that my self-consumption often drives me away from experiencing the beauty found in the community garden of the Lord, where loving and appreciating others actually gives life to me. May I learn better not only to appreciate your garden, but may I be an active contributor of love to your garden as well. For your name's sake. Amen!

QUESTIONS FOR YOU TO PONDER

- So have I allowed myself to prefer "aloneness" over and above the God-breathed life available to me in and through community with others?
- Am I willing to lay down some of my personal drive to prefer and defer to the type of community Jesus desires for his church?

So, what is God speaking to you today as you ponder the *Wisdom of Wimber*?

KOINONIA

The New Testament, written in Greek, contains some words that are difficult to translate and for which there are no exact English equivalents. This language barrier creates challenges for Christians who want to think and live biblically.

The Greek word that is commonly translated "fellowship" (*koinonia* - see Acts 4:32 and 1 John 1:3) is perhaps the best example of this. Koinonia implies far more than socializing at church potlucks or chatting on the church's front lawn after Sunday service. The word means "holding our lives in common," a meaning that first century Christians demonstrated through spiritual, social, and material generosity toward one another.

Fellowship (is) a "common sharing of the grace and of the blessings of God," a definition that comes close to the biblical idea of koinonia.[32]

All churches associated with John Wimber and the Vineyard were originally called Vineyard Christian Fellowships. When Sandy and I started our church plant in Iowa City in 1988, and then again in Cedar Rapids in 1998, it was required that new churches take the name "Vineyard Christian Fellowship" to be officially associated with the Vineyard family.

Today, that name has disappeared almost completely from the Vineyard, with most churches (including our own here in Cedar Rapids) changing their names to "Vineyard Church of such-and-such city." At the time we changed our name, most Vineyard pastors reasoned that the general public just didn't really know what a "fellowship" was anymore, and with the cultural resistance to any word (i.e., fellow) that might represent any sexual bias, it seemed wise to dump the word "fellowship" and just call ourselves a "church."

Hmm.

I know that this might sound like some old pastor who pines for the good-old-days, but after reading John's quote here on *koinonia*, I'm wondering, if by changing our names away from "fellowship," we might have also allowed our churches to wander away from the truest definitions of community as described in the New Testament?

As Wimber states here, *koinonia* means so much more than folks coming through the doors on Sunday morning, sitting in a chair while staring at a stage full of activity, sipping coffee with a handful of people sitting next to you, and making light conversation before grabbing the kids and heading out the door into another week of work, school, and life.

I've talked with several other pastors of both larger churches and smaller churches in our area and the results are pretty much the same. They believe life-giving small groups, where people (using Wimber's definition of *koinonia*) experience "a common sharing of the grace and of the blessings of God" is a rare thing indeed. This is why, I believe, we're seeing more and more experimentation with "doing church" across America today. My friend, Bill Faris, has been a Vineyard pastor in southern California for decades. Several years ago, he came to a growing awareness that his traditional Vineyard church was not producing the kind of *koinonia* Wimber talks about here. Recently, he wrote the following commentary about some of his recent experiences as they've been using a different church model on Sunday mornings. Here is what he said:

> I often tell people about our House Church when I am out and about. It is not uncommon for people to sound interested in making a visit to see what all this is about. Sometimes I think: "they wouldn't necessarily be very impressed" by what they saw. Let me explain.
>
> In my more traditional church ministry days it was very much on my mind to seek to impress visitors. In fact it was important to do so because, often, they were either "church shopping" or otherwise in the "we are checking you out" column. Nowadays, it's more like having someone over to be with my family. Our attitude at House

Church is: "you're welcome here. Come and be a part of our family and make yourself comfortable".

Imagine, then, if you went to visit someone's family and they had a greeter at the front door who handed you a piece of paper that had the schedule of what your hangout time with the family consisted of. Then imagine that someone walked you into the living room and told you where you should probably sit. Someone else asked you if you were "new" at the Faris House and if you had any questions, etc. Wouldn't that feel odd? Trust me, I understand why people make special efforts to do things a certain way at "Big Church". But this is not the House Church way.

To be sure, we have some structure and there is leadership in action at our meetings. But how "impressive" is it (in that certain sense of the term) that a 10 year old led our worship on the piano as best as she could last Sunday? Believe me: I loved it and it feels so right to have the children of the kingdom minister at their capacity and from their hearts. Phil Strout, our new National Director in the Vineyard, is very strong on enrolling the next generations into the life and practice of God's kingdom. But no "Big Church" would feature 10 year old Stephanie at the keys on a Sunday a.m. I was happy for Stephanie that, after practicing all week and taking it seriously, she *knew* she would be followed and received by the adults as our worship leader of the week last Sunday. There is something very sweet and very good about this.

Then, I listened as Steve Bagley recounted his remarkable adventures in ministry. It was clear that our notion that our people "take us with them" when they minister away from Foothill Ranch is absolutely the case. I love this discovery we've made of this concept. It was fantastic to feel the sense of partnership we had in Steve's trip, especially after just finishing up our Christmas shopping efforts for the Philippines. Then listening to Kristen explain about Stacey and Jessica and the Berkeley Students For Life and knowing that we could participate in "sending" Kristen and Stacey to be with Jessica (one of our "at large" House Church members!) was, again, "impressive" to me. Sharing in Melodie and Kathy's victories in the workplace and rejoicing in Melodie's encouraging reports about Nicole — impressive!

And having Steve Bashford there on his own with his son, Jacob — and watching a four year old come in, make himself at home, and watching how Stephanie instantly started reaching out to him and caring for him and knowing that Danielle has already been babysitting him and feeling his comfort with her — all quite impressive. And knowing that Robert was in Japan but not far from our hearts and knowing that Hsiwen could share the big news of his becoming an Uncle again and me sharing about what God is doing in my life with a roomful of people who I now see as essential to his work through me — again, impressive!

Yet, just as Jesus had "no form that we should desire him" (Isaiah 53) and was not "impressive" in carnal ways and yet carried the power, anointing, mission, and presence of God in his person — this is what House Church reminds me. The Incarnation was not razzle dazzle. It was God touching real people in real, simple, and profound ways as he demonstrated his love and executed his plan to save and heal us. Impressive? Yes — but not in worldly ways.

So, with these thoughts I'll close this meditation for now. So much more could be said. We were so full of things to share about how God was working in our lives last Sunday we could scarcely get the teaching time regarding the Intro to Proverbs (but we did). That may not be "impressive" in a technical and scheduled sense, but I think it really pleases the Lord that we have become so mutually-supportive and integrated into one another's walks with Christ that we don't dare meet just to get other stuff done for its own sake. We take time to "be with". Would all this impress the visitor who thinks (perhaps) House Church is the hip "new thing"? Perhaps not. When it comes down to it, we are not all that "impressive" (on the outside) — and yet, to those who have eyes and ears for the kingdom of God — there is a lot more to us than anyone would have ever guessed. And that is impressive![33]

Thanks, Bill. As I see it, what you guys and gals are presently experiencing at your Vineyard House Church sure sounds a lot more like what John Wimber defined as biblical *koinonia*. There are hundreds of stories out there like this. What's your story? Find someone and share it.

PRAYER

Father God, I feel the conviction of the Holy Spirit. I'm sad that to become an established church, we've lost much of the fellowship that we set out to do in the process. *Koinonia,* Jesus, is not just an ancient word to be studied, but is a Spirit-empowered activity to be explored. Help me, Father, to find creative new ways to stir true *koinonia* in our midst. For your name's sake. Amen!

QUESTIONS FOR YOU TO PONDER

- What ministry decisions have we made in our churches that have actually served to reduce *koinonia* (fellowship) amongst the people? Is it possible to restore biblical "fellowship" in a generation where social media has become our primary tool of communication?
- If so, what specifics might God be asking of me and my church to accomplish this goal?

So, what is God speaking to you today as you ponder the *Wisdom of Wimber?*

Fellowship begins with a relationship with Jesus Christ. In John 14: 6-15, Jesus says to the apostles, "I am the way and the truth and the life. No one comes to the Father, but through me." Most Christians, even baby Christians, are familiar with this passage of Scripture. In many instances this is the passage through which they were led to put their faith in Christ! "If you want to know the Father," Jesus says, "you must know me."

But few Christians realize it is also a truth that informs us about the basis for our relationship with brothers and sisters. Philip is confused about what Jesus says. "Lord," Philip asks, "show us the Father and that will be enough for us." Jesus answers, "Don't you know me, Philip?...Anyone who has seen me has seen the Father."

This is one of the most profound and important teachings in Scripture. Jesus and the Father are one and always have been one. The theologians would say that they are one in nature, though they are two distinct persons. Jesus said only words that the Father told him to say; he did only deeds the Father told him to do; he performed only works that the Father performed.

The Father was so pleased with him that even before Jesus began his public ministry, at his baptism, he split the heavens and spoke saying, "This is my kid, and I really like him. I really approve of him. I am pleased with him."

And Jesus has invited us into this same quality of relationship. So the basis for knowing and experiencing fellowship with brothers and sisters is entering a relationship with the Father through the Son. Fellowship with brothers and sisters for early

Christians was a result and an expression of their fellowship with God in Christ and in the Holy Spirit (see 1 Cor. 1:9; Phil. 2:1; 1 John 1:3).[34]

Sadly, so many of us earth-dwellers try to do really good things out of our own strength.

Take "community," for example.

Today, there is a growing movement to build stronger and healthier community-living across the USA called Blue Zones. Author Dan Buettner and his book *The Blue Zones: Lessons for Living Longer from People Who Lived the Longest*[35] identifies several longevity hotspots across the planet and offers an explanation, based on empirical data and firsthand observations, as to why these populations live healthier and longer lives. Buettner's organization has now developed a specific list of life-style changes people can make to live longer, healthier, and better lives. My city of Cedar Rapids, Iowa, has taken that list and is now offering educational and information resources, health programs, foods and food services, real estate developments, and consumer goods to those in our area who are interested in seeing our community become, yet another, Blue Zone.

Now don't get me wrong.

I like the list of life-style changes offered by Buettner. If you are interested, you can watch his convincing TED talk.[36] I found it intriguing that one of the key lessons discovered in the Blue Zone study is that there is a powerful element released into our human existence when people choose to live together in close community. And when that tight-knit community, Buettner states, is focused around a common spiritual belief with corresponding actions that live out that shared belief, the benefits to life, in general, are very impressive, indeed.

Hmm. Seems to me that I read in the New Testament about that same "upward life" theme as the Good News about Jesus spread across the Roman Empire during the first century!

But here's the rub.

Here in my city, a growing number of Christians are very excited about Cedar Rapids becoming a Blue Zone community. I'd like to share in their unbridled excitement, but quite honestly, our local Blue Zone organization has, from my perspective, screened out all references to God and spirituality (which, of course, shouldn't surprise me) and places all the energy to accomplish good at the feet of human effort.

Over my lifetime, I've seen way too many good people try to accomplish many good things through the power of their own wills. How often have I seen well-meaning Christians attempt to live in "community," believing it to be the biblical way, but fail to realize that true *koinonia* (community) happens only when Jesus, the Christ, is appointed leader of such an entity?

You see, Wimber was right. The early church understood that when they formed *koinonia* (shared community), it had to be built exclusively around the Son of God. Christ-centeredness is not just a theology but a day-to-day practice that must be lived out if you and I ever hope to form a successful "community" that will truly last.

So, making my city into a Blue Zone. Sure. I say, let's go for it, fellow Cedar Rapidians. But let's understand that it will have its limits. The same limits will most likely be in your community as well.

Count me in. Let's learn to practice healthy lifestyles, eat better foods, and treat one another much better than we currently do. But as for me and my household, any real Blue Zone I want to be permanently tied to must be one where the agreed center is Jesus of Nazareth. Call me a cynic, but somehow I just don't think any secularized approach to "community," where we all just try to get along, is gonna happen without him!

PRAYER

Father God, it seems as though every generation comes up with their own great ideas on how to make civilization behave. But in all honesty, trying to live in successful community without the full leadership of Jesus of Nazareth at the center of that community will ultimately fail. Holy Spirit, as my generation tries, once again, to find peace on earth through the exertion of human will, may I be found looking to you for the answers we all seek. For your name's sake. Amen!

Question To Ponder

- How can I cooperatively involve myself with good human efforts like Blue Zones and other positive approaches to life, placing my hand to help bring an upward lift to my community while never sacrificing my own personal belief that Jesus of Nazareth is the only gateway to true community (*koinonia*)?
- With these guidelines, how is your community healthy or unhealthy?

So, what is God speaking to you today as you ponder the *Wisdom of Wimber?*

It's All About Relationship

The biblical concept of fellowship is important to understand and live out. In the early church there was a relationship between the warmth of heart toward God and generosity toward each other. So close were these relationships the early Christians did not see themselves as isolated individuals but as "members one of another," in "communities" where individuals grew to spiritual maturity and cooperated with each other in advancing God's kingdom. Within these communities they gained strength, support, and protection from the corroding influences of the world. Thus they were well prepared to face anything the devil might throw at them when they went out into the world.

This quality of relationship contrasts sharply with many modern Christians' faith, which narrow their relationship with God to individualistic concerns like repentance and conversion, prayer and Scripture study, personal righteousness and evangelism. But God has called us to grow to maturity in the body of Christ. We are called to "attain to the unity of the faith and of the knowledge of the Son of God," growing up "in every way into him who is the head, into God, from whom the whole body, joined and knit together by every joint with which it is supplied, when each part is working properly, makes bodily growth and upbuilds itself in love" (Eph. 4:13, 15-16).[37]

There's a problem in Americanized Christianity that continues to haunt me as a pastoral shepherd. I think the problem haunted John Wimber as well.

That problem, as I see it, is the fierce independent spirit of most Americans and how that drive for independence fights against God's desire to see his people walk out their Christian faith in the context of long-term, loving, nurturing relationships.

Now, don't get me wrong. Independence, or our freedom to be ourselves, is, at its very core, a gift from God. Quite honestly, our freedom to make choices independent from outside influence is a gift most people in the world would die for. In fact, countless Americans have given their very lives, over the years, defending that freedom we have to be independent people.

But every gift from God is like a sharp razor. In the hands of a skilled barber, the sharp edge can give us a great shave. But, put that same razor in the hands of an immature, inexperienced man, and the consequences can literally take your life.

So it is with the gift of independence.

Over the last thirty years of pastoral ministry, overseeing church life in four different churches in three different cities, I'm guessing that I've had the privilege to meet literally hundreds and hundreds (if not thousands) of Christians who have come through the doors of the churches I've pastored. Sadly, the great majority of these committed followers of Christ that I've met over my thirty years in ministry have rarely stayed at our church for much longer than a few months to a few years. In fact, a running joke amongst pastors is the one about the new visitor who comes up after a Sunday morning service and proudly proclaims, "Pastor, this is great! God has told me that *your* church is the place where I *really* belong!" Sadly, it's been most pastor's experiences that folks who say nice things like that, usually leave the church within a few weeks!

Now, some would say that church life is not about keeping people. And, in premise, I agree. But here's the sad fact. Most American Christians rarely put down any long-term, relational roots. Our independent spirit so very often pushes us to move on, believing that the next church we attend will meet all of our needs, or the next pastor we listen to will speak to us as we want him or her to, or the next small group will be the one where we'll settle down.

Let's face it folks. The New Testament concept of community, as Wimber spells it out here, is foreign to most American churches. The idea of relationships as being "members one of another, in communities where individuals grow to spiritual maturity and

112

cooperate with each other in God's kingdom" is about as hard to find in our churches today as a one-hundred dollar bill in a collection plate!

Now before you write off my thoughts here as just another old pastor who's been hurt badly by people leaving his church over the years, let me give you a few statistics pulled from recent church growth studies:

- Every year more than 4,000 churches close their doors compared to just over 1,000 new church starts.
- Every year 2.7 million church members fall into inactivity.
- Over the last decade, the combined membership of all Protestant denominations in the USA declined by almost 5 million members (9.5 percent), while the US population increased by 24 million (11 percent).
- At the beginning of the twentieth century (1900), there was a ratio of twenty-seven churches per 10,000 people, as compared to the close of twentieth century (2000) where there were only eleven churches per 10,000 people in America.
- Half of all churches in the US did not add any new members to their ranks in the last two years.[38]

Sadly, our independent spirit here in America, when combined with our fierce drive for self-entitlement, has brought us, as westernized Christians, to a place where "church as usual" is just not cutting it anymore. Statistics show that more and more people, after "trying out" a few churches in their area, finally just decide to stay at home and follow Jesus by themselves. All the while, church growth experts sell "how to" books to pastors, encouraging church leaders to work both smarter and harder at developing more creative programming to keep the masses from leaving our pews.

Hmm.

When will the madness stop?

Sadly, I'm not a predictor of the future, but I am a reader of the New Testament. In Matthew's gospel (Matthew 24: 10-14), we find Jesus saying these very hard truths:

At that time many will turn away from the faith and will betray and hate each other, and many false prophets will appear and deceive many people. Because of the increase of wickedness, the love of most will grow cold, but the one who stands firm to the end will be saved. And this gospel of the kingdom will be preached in the whole world as a testimony to all nations, and then the end will come.

Are we at such a time as this? Only God knows., From my perspective, it just might be time for God's appointed leaders to stop playing games, trying our very best to excite and entertain the crowds, and morph ourselves back into being New Testament pastors and shepherds whose job is to call God's people back into true community, where we all lay down our fleshly, self-centered wills of independence so that God might give us his gift of *koinonia* (long-term, loving, nurturing community) for the rough times ahead.

PRAYER

Father God, cutting edge Christianity has always been, at its very core, all about relationships, long-term, loving, nurturing relationship with you and long-term, loving, nurturing relationship with fellow believers. Spirit, bring your church back again to these simple things. For your name's sake. Amen!

QUESTIONS FOR YOU TO PONDER

- What must I do to step away from the typical way we Americans look at church life and our commitment to such things?
- What might it look like for a handful of committed followers of Christ to lay down our fleshly, self-consumed independence while picking up Christ's servant-hood attitude toward others?
- Is it possible in our current society to step into a counter-culture of long-term, loving, nurturing relationships?
- And if so, what might it look like for me to participate with such things?

So, what is God speaking to you today as you ponder the *Wisdom of Wimber?*

KINSHIP IN THE EARLY CHURCH

We are...called to community, a sharing of help, gifts, resources, and problems. The early Christians often met in
one another's homes, ate together, and took a practical concern for each other's material needs (Acts 4:32). They helped
each other with life's many difficulties, "bearing each other's
burdens and ... fulfilling the law of Christ" (Gal. 6:2).

Because of this closeness the early church was careful about
conversational patterns like slander and gossip, recogniz-
ing how dangerous out of control tongues can be. They also
knew how to keep confidences and protect each other.

How were they able to live out this type of closeness? It appears they facilitated a common life through small groups,
such as the churches that met in homes (Rom. 15:5, 14-15;
1 Thess. 5:27; Col. 4:15). Small groups are also the basis for
Christian community today.

Paul, in Ephesians 4:2, says, "Be completely humble and
gentle with one another in love." I have often thought,
How can people love each other if they never relate personally?
That is the point of small groups, they are where people can
relate, can actually live out the gospel. In small groups we
learn how to love the unlovely, thus fulfilling the command
of Christ. Sometimes we are the ones in need of special love
and support to get us through difficult times.[39]

In the beginning days of the Vineyard, small groups were
called "kinship" groups. The word "kinship" has, for the
most part, been lost in today's church culture, but it might
not be a bad idea to re-look at this word to see if we can

restore a stronger aspect of community (*koinonia*) into our churches today.

Kinship is defined in dictionaries as "a connection by blood, marriage, or adoption; a family relationship." As Wimber states here, small groups (kinship) is a place where folks can share "help, gifts, resources and problems" with one another.

Did you know that the New Testament writers share that you and I, as followers of Christ, are called to the concepts of kinship? Actually the New Testament Greek root word is *allelon*, and it is translated as "one another" or "each other." Here are a few of those "one another" texts. Take a deep breath. Here we go:

1. "Be at peace with each other." (Mark 9:50)
2. "Wash one another's feet." (John 13:14)
3. "Love one another" (John 13:34, 35, 15:12, 17, Romans 13: 8, 1 John 3:11, 23, 4:7, 11, 12, 2 John 5)
4. "Be devoted to one another in brotherly love" (Romans 12:10)
5. "Honor one another above yourselves." (Romans 12:10)
6. "Live in harmony with one another" (Romans 12:16)
7. "Stop passing judgment on one another." (Romans 14:13)
8. "Accept one another, then, just as Christ accepted you" (Romans 15:7)
9. "Instruct one another." (Romans 15:14)
10. "Greet one another with a holy kiss" (Romans 16:16, 1 Corinthians 16:20, 2 Corinthians 13:12)
11. "When you come together to eat, wait for each other." (1 Corinthians 11:33)
12. "Have equal concern for each other." (1 Corinthians 12:25)
13. "Serve one another in love." (Galatians 5:13)
14. "Carry each other's burdens" (Galatians 6:2)
15. "Be patient, bearing with one another in love." (Ephesians 4:2)
16. "Be kind and compassionate to one another" (Ephesians 4:32)
17. "Forgiving each other" (Ephesians 4:32, Colossians 3:13)

18. "Speak to one another with psalms, hymns and spiritual songs." (Ephesians 5:19)
19. "Submit to one another out of reverence for Christ." (Ephesians 5:21)
20. "In humility consider others better than yourselves." (Philippians 2:3)
21. "Do not lie to each other" (Colossians 3:9)
22. "Bear with each other" (Colossians 3:13)
23. "Teach...[one another]" (Colossians 3:16)
24. "Admonish one another (Colossians 3:16)
25. "Make your love increase and overflow for each other." (1 Thessalonians 3:12)
26. "Encourage each other" (1 Thessalonians 4:18, 5:11, Hebrews 3: 13, 10:25)
27. "Build each other up" (1 Thessalonians 5:11)
28. "Spur one another on toward love and good deeds." (Hebrews 10:24)
29. "Do not slander one another." (James 4:11)
30. "Don't grumble against each other" (James 5:9)
31. "Confess your sins to each other" (James 5:16)
32. "Pray for each other." (James 5:16)
33. "Love one another deeply, from the heart." (1 Peter 3:8, 4:8)
34. "Live in harmony with one another" (1 Peter 3:8)
35. "Offer hospitality to one another without grumbling." (1 Peter 4:9)
36. "Each one should use whatever gift he has received to serve others" (1 Peter 4:10)
37. "Clothe yourselves with humility toward one another" (1 Peter 5:5)
38. "Greet one another with a kiss of love." (1 Peter 5:14)

'Nuff said.

PRAYER

Jesus, it will take a lifetime for me to become biblically obedient to just these 'one-another' texts of the New Testament. Forgive me,

Lord, when I stray from these commands and place other ministries and works of the church over and above these powerful calls to kinship. Holy Spirit, indwell and empower your church to fulfill these words in my generation. For your name's sake. Amen!

QUESTIONS FOR YOU TO PONDER

- What might church look like if we started to take these thirty-eight "one-another" commands of the New Testament and started to act upon them, placing them at the top of our "to-do" lists in ministry?
- Where am I failing to follow these commands, allowing other worldly activities to trump these simple instructions to *agape* (unconditionally love) *allelon* (one-another)?

So, what is God speaking to you today as you ponder the *Wisdom of Wimber?*

> (A true) measurement of disciples is whether the church life is at the center of their life.
>
> Loving Christ is only part of the picture. We also need to love what he loves, which is the church. Disciples love the church because God loves the church. He doesn't look down from heaven and see divisions of churches. He sees a bride preparing herself for marriage to his Son. The church is the only thing Jesus is coming back for.
>
> If the people who come to our churches only get connected with Christ, they may or may not stay. But if they get connected with Christ and with other brothers and sisters in Christ, they'll probably stay – unless the Lord moves them out. They're looking for relationship and identity. They're looking for reality and something that will get them through life.[40]

As we read Wimber's quote here on discipleship, I envision true Christian community as being very similar to a three-pronged electrical plug. Let me walk you briefly through each of the three important components, as I see them:

Connectedness to Christ

The first and most important prong of Christian community represents our secure alignment with Christ. Without a primary focus on Jesus of Nazareth, our community experiences will be nothing more than a commitment to some sort of a social organization. Sadly, many Americans attend church out of a sense of duty or possibly because of a need to be seen or heard, thus too many churches become not much more than a country club where membership revolves around what I referenced earlier as the 3-Bs: where we measure success by the size of (B)uildings, the stack of (B)ucks in the offering, and the number of (B)utts in the seats. John Wimber firmly believed that any Christian church must be Christ-centered, with Jesus of Nazareth becoming the power source behind any successful attempt at community.

CONNECTEDNESS TO OTHERS

The second prong of Christian community represents our firm connectedness to one another. As we discussed in the last section, there are dozens of references in the New Testament where Christ-centered people are commanded to love one another; living sacrificial lives that prefer others over and above our own selfish interests. Casual commitments to fellow believers just didn't exist in the New Testament church and John Wimber would often remind pastors within the Vineyard movement that it was relatively easy to gather a crowd, but vastly different to actually birth a church community. To Wimber, there was a huge difference between groups of loosely connected people (a crowd) versus an assembled gathering of disciples (a *real* church).

GROUNDED IN LOVE

All electrical plugs in our homes have two prongs conducting the electricity that flows from the power source (the outlet in the wall) to the appliance or tool being used. The first electrical wire conducts the positive (incoming) flow of electricity, while the other conducts the negative (outgoing) flow. So it is with Christian community. Our incoming power always comes from Jesus Christ, the ultimate source of energy throughout the universe; while our outgoing commitment to others empowers all we call Christian mission. Disconnect either one of these two wires and our appliance called Christian community just won't work! Remember this. All UL-tested and approved electrical plugs sold in the USA and Canada must also include, by law, a third prong called the grounding wire. As I see it, the grounding wire in all Christian community is *agape*: unconditional love, received from heaven above and then given away freely to others around us. Jesus spelled it out this way in his powerful prayer found in John 17: 20-23 (NIV):

> My prayer is not for them alone. I pray also for those who will believe in me through their message, that all of them may be one, Father, just as you are in me and I am in you. May they also be in us so that the world may believe that you have sent me. I have given them the glory that you gave me, that they may be one as we are one—I in them and you in me—so that they may be brought to complete unity. Then the world will know that you sent me and have loved them even as you have loved me.

So there you have it. True Christian community! It is a connectedness to Christ and a connectedness to others with agape love grounding everything we say and do.

Now, all we have to do, my fellow Christian disciples, is stop twiddling our thumbs as we sit idly in the pews, get up out of our seats, and plug our "Christian community" appliance into the wall socket to make *all* the lights come on!

And the light coming from that flame can truly light the world!

PRAYER

The life-changing power of true Christian community is amazing, God. It worked well in the early church, I believe you can make it work well today. I choose, Master, to do my part. I want to become totally connected to Christ, completely connected to others, while allowing your agape love to ground us along the way. For your name's sake. Amen!

QUESTIONS FOR YOU TO PONDER

- Where is there a loose connection in my wiring when it comes to true Christian community? Am I fully connected with Jesus of Nazareth or is my relationship on a hit-and-miss basis? What about my connectedness to my brothers and sisters in Christ?

- Is it in words alone or am I doing all Jesus asks of me in connecting with others? Finally, is agape love grounding all of my relationships, both my relationship with God and my relationships with others?

So, what is God speaking to you today as you ponder the *Wisdom of Wimber?*

True Christian community! It is a connectedness
to Christ and a connectedness to others...

ON COMPASSION

Jesus came down to earth. I didn't go up to him.

LIVING IN BROKENNESS

The church is represented in my life. I'm not all that Jesus wants me to be. I'm not all that he's provided for me. I'm not walking in all that I know. I'm trying, but I'm not doing all that well some days. Are you? That leaves me in a broken state — an awareness of, "O God, O God, except for your mercy and except for your grace." I think it's designed to be that way. I think we are supposed to live in the constant reality that we are not measuring up. Even in his righteousness, even under his mercy, even as a recipient of his grace, I can't walk like Jesus does. I touch on it every now and then. I visit it. That gives me hope and encouragement for more. But the reality is that we have to constantly live in brokenness. The way we do that, is by not developing some sort of external religious thing that hides us and puts us in a denial process by which we pretend to be more than we are. Rather, we just learn to live constantly with the awareness that we just don't measure up.

But that's good news, folks. If you don't measure up — if you *can't* measure up — then you're constantly asking for Jesus to make up the difference. That's good news! It's pretty hard to act overly religious when you know you don't measure up, and that he's paying the difference. I'm not sure that we ever get incredibly better or stronger or mightier, becoming these great men and women of God. I think we always live with the awareness that we are serving the great God of men and women. Jesus came down to earth. I didn't go up to him. He came to the world. The world didn't come to him. I got saved by a merciful Savior. Didn't you? And he's still merciful toward me. Every day of my life I live in a constant awareness of that.[41]

To John Wimber, a church was not a true church if that group of people wasn't acting "otherly," giving of themselves to the poor, the needy, the outcast, and the lost. Thus, when Wimber gave his Genetic Code talk to Vineyard pastors in 1991, where he listed ten areas of ministry that he believed to be essentials for any church who hoped to be a "doin' the stuff" kind of church; number five on that list was: "a ministry to the poor, widows, orphans, and those who are broken."

As you can read from the quote above, Wimber understood that brokenness was part and parcel with all life lived here on planet earth. And it was this theology of brokenness that formed so much of who he was and the way he consciously acted toward himself and toward others. Brokenness, you see, is the key to understanding the plight of our human existence.

In the beginning, when Adam and Eve first decided that they knew better than God and that they didn't need the Creator's help in making major decisions in their lives, it was their inability to see themselves as broken that pushed them to choose the way they did. You see, Satan knows that he has no chance to lure us into his snares as long as we remain broken and dependent upon God for our strength. So when the serpent was tempting Adam and Eve, he was simply puffing up the human spirit, making them believe that they knew as much about life as God did.

As I see it, there's nothing worse than human beings who refuse to embrace their brokenness. Pride, arrogance, and self-centeredness are, quite honestly, at the very center of our human existence outside God. And it's our refusal to admit to that brokenness that so often keeps people from truly experiencing the tender-hearted mercies of God.

Let's face it folks, well-meaning Christians who are full of themselves, victorious, and free, can end up being some of the most repulsive people in the world to be around! Why? It is because our failure to see ourselves as broken people, as Wimber states, can remove our one hundred percent reliance upon God as being our Savior. And when that happens, all ministries we attempt to do for Jesus becomes a mixture of our good intentions and our self-centered pride trying to blend together with the total sufficiency and complete sovereignty of God. And just like oil being stirred into water, those two elements: human pride combined with God's will; just never blend into one!

So the key to successful ministries of compassion, then, is our ability to, first and foremost, see ourselves as broken people serving other broken people. Equals to those we are hoping to help. I love the way author Henri Nouwen defined it. In this world, as we go in God's compassion to others, we're simply, "wounded healers." We are simply broken people with a great Savior going to other broken people in need of that same great Savior.

So what do you say that we stop the ministries of compassion that are going out of our churches in the name of our victorious human abilities? How about if we check our pride and arrogance at the door the next time we're prepping to go out to help the less fortunate and go only in the name and power of Jesus, alone? Somehow I think that approach, ministering compassion out of his strength and out of our own brokenness, will play much better in a world where everybody seems to enjoy helping others, especially when they can get all the credit and publicity for doing such good things.

PRAYER

Father, in all truthfulness, I'm a broken man always in need of a great Savior. Help me as I attempt to go to others in your compassion. May I never go to assist others while I'm full of myself and may your Holy Spirit grant me the joy of giving grace to others in need while I, myself, always remain a recipient of your grace as well. For your name's sake. Amen!

QUESTIONS FOR YOU TO PONDER

- Am I fully aware of my continual brokenness in the sight of God?
- How can I better embrace that brokenness, knowing that it's in my weakness that I am strong?
- How might my outreach toward others be strengthened as I choose to go in my brokenness, believing that it's his

strength that actually makes the true difference in all of our lives?

So, what is God speaking to you today as you ponder the *Wisdom of Wimber*?

THE REALITY OF POVERTY

We in the American church have (a) problem that clouds our perspective on the reality of poverty. Because of our culturally-derived attitudes, we've emphasized the "right" of Christians to be prosperous to the de-emphasis of ministry to the oppressed poor. Scripture does indicate that the redeemed of the Lord will prosper. In Church Growth terminology this is called "Redemption and Lift." Once a people or community has been largely redeemed, there will be a dimension of social-economic lift that is measurable over a few generations. So while it is true that we can expect to prosper, there is a PURPOSE for our prosperity. We have become a part of the redemptive plan of God in meeting the needs of people less fortunate than we are as a community and as a people.[42]

Poverty, as defined in a dictionary, is the state of one who lacks a certain amount of material possessions or money. In a larger sense, poverty is the inability to obtain choices and opportunities, a violation of human dignity. It means not having the basic capacity to participate effectively in society: not having enough to feed and clothe a family, not having a school or clinic to go to, or not having the land on which to grow one's food and/or a job to earn one's living. Poverty means insecurity, powerlessness and exclusion of individuals, households, and communities. Sadly, it also means a certain susceptibility to violence, and it often implies living in marginal or fragile environments, without access to clean water or sanitation. Groups who study poverty around the world use the term "absolute poverty" that refers to the deprivation of basic human needs, which commonly includes food, water, sanitation, clothing, shelter, health care, and education. In 2008, the World Bank estimated that 1.29 billion people on our planet exist in "absolute poverty."

The opposite of poverty is prosperity. Those living in prosperity, then, will have ready access to all those same basic needs that those living in poverty don't. So simply said, our world ends up being divided into two groups; the "haves" and the "have nots." Sadly, this mismatch of opportunity has been with us here on planet earth for a very long time. Those who "have," when left to their own devices, tend to stay that way, while the "have nots" will tend to stay in poverty as well. On the good side, recent reports tell us that between 1990 and 2010, approximately 663 million people moved above the absolute poverty level for the first time! But sadly, extreme poverty remains a global challenge and, as Jesus so accurately pointed out to his disciples, "you will always have the poor in your midst."

Every generation of Christians since the day Jesus first stated the obvious, has had to wrestle with the very difficult questions surrounding poverty and prosperity. As Wimber said, world history shows us that the Good News of Jesus, when lived out within a society for many years, does tend to bring an upward lift to that society. Indeed, God desires his people to prosper, and as a people following Jesus and his commands, it's true that poverty is reduced in that society where the kingdom of God flourishes. I like the way Wimber states it. In the economy of God, "there is specific purpose to prosperity." From a biblical perspective, all wealth and material blessings (i.e., prosperity) come from the hand of God. Sadly, many people, including many Christians, often forget this fact, giving themselves the credit for their ability to accumulate great wealth or earthly success. So when a godly man or woman prospers, it's vitally important in the economies of God's kingdom, then, for that same prosperous person to always remember, in generosity, the poor; giving back to those in poverty a healthy portion of wealth so that all on the community may be blessed.

Generosity, you see, is a gift of the Holy Spirit. A man or woman can operate in generosity even though they might be living in prosperity or poverty. In fact, I've met some folks living near poverty levels who operate more in the gift of generosity than those who have been blessed with great prosperity! So the key then, whether a person lives in prosperity or in poverty, is to become a generous person. And a generous person, working under the unction of the Holy Spirit, can change a lot of earthy circumstances in amazing ways. Pastor Chuck Swindoll had a marvelous teaching on this subject. He called it "Hilarious Generosity"[43] and he said that when a person begins living in the grace of generosity, it becomes nearly laughable in the way a generous person can bring great joy in the midst of great suffering.

So there you have it, my friends. May the Lord of the Harvest, who offers us his bounty of prosperity, also grant to us his hilarious gift of generosity. As I see it, with it, the poverty levels around the world could take yet another big hit in the days to come!

PRAYER

Father God, poverty is, without a doubt, a condition birthed in the pits of hell. No one should have to live in the grips of poverty and if we, your people, can become an increasingly generous people, led by your Spirit, many, many more, who are presently living in absolute poverty, can be lifted out of that hell-hole. For your name's sake. Amen!

QUESTION FOR YOU TO PONDER

- Am I closing my eyes to the plight of the poor?
- Has alleviating poverty become such an overwhelming task that it's easier for me to just ignore the subject while enjoying my prosperity?
- What level is my generosity at this moment? What might it look like to become "hilarious" with my generosity?

So, what is God speaking to you today as you ponder the *Wisdom of Wimber?*

MESSIAH'S JOB DESCRIPTION

Throughout history, because of the sin and greed of man and the work of Satan, human economic, social and religious institutions have been tainted and often work to enslave and oppress the very people they were set up to serve or govern. Many poor people are not only victims of their own misguided lifestyles, they are also victims of institutional oppression. Because of the tyranny of these forces, people are driven from their places within society to a poverty level - unable to care for themselves.

Jesus graphically identified with the poor people of his day. He spent most of his public ministry time with people in the market places and streets, rubbing elbows with the sick, sinners and the poor, seeking to liberate them from whatever enslaved them. Jesus can give us courage to minister to the poor in our day. He can open our eyes to see the oppressed poor in our community and give us direction as how to best minister to their needs.[44]

A t the very beginning of Jesus' three-year ministry, our Master made it very clear why he had come. Luke's gospel spells it out for us precisely in his fourth chapter, and if you hung around John Wimber for any length of time, it wouldn't be long before Luke 4: 18-19 came rolling off his tongue.

Here in Luke's writings, Jesus of Nazareth, now fully indwelled and empowered in the Holy Spirit, has just returned from his grueling desert wilderness experience, and is now beginning to teach in the synagogues of Galilee. Luke tells us that on the day he was attending Sabbath services in his hometown of Nazareth, he was invited to read the Scripture of the day. The scrolls were opened to what we refer to as Isaiah 61 and Jesus read the following words:

> The Spirit of the Lord is on me,
>   because he has anointed me
>   to proclaim good news to the poor.
> He has sent me to proclaim freedom for the prisoners
>   and recovery of sight for the blind,
> to set the oppressed free,
>   to proclaim the year of the Lord's favor (Luke 4:18-19).

In synagogue worship settings, it's customary for all the men to stand during the reading of the Scriptures, after which all are seated. After everyone has taken their seats, the reader of the text is given the honor of speaking first; giving his insights and thoughts about the text that has just been read. This is why Luke tells us that all eyes were fixed on Jesus after he had read this messianic passage from Isaiah.

I'm sure that most of the men in the synagogue that day were expecting Jesus to do what all rabbi-wannabes would do after reading this familiar text. Since everyone knew that this passage in Isaiah 61 is referencing the dramatic changes that will occur in society when the Messiah arrives, I'm guessing that most were expecting Jesus, the hometown boy, to say a few kind words and then turn the proceedings over to the eldest rabbi, so that he could lead the discussion with the men.

But on this typical Saturday afternoon, the synagogue service in Nazareth took a turn literally no one (except, maybe Jesus?) expected. Luke tells us that indeed, the Master didn't talk very long, but what he did say was so outrageous, it blew the meeting apart, ending it in a near riot. He stated: "Today, this scripture is fulfilled in your hearing."

The way Luke's text reads, I'm thinking that Jesus must have said this sentence in a sweet tone, because apparently, a few folks smiled at first, thinking kindly of the nice young man they had known growing up in Nazareth. But then, after a few more choice comments, the crowd finally started to realize what Jesus had actually said. Before long, they've taken Jesus out of church and are ready to throw him off a cliff!

I've heard Dr. Don Williams, a good friend of John Wimber and a man well-trained in Hebrew thought, explain that Jesus' eight-word sentence here would be very similar to someone standing up in one of our churches today and saying to the crowd…"This passage of Scripture I've just read is being fulfilled today…by me…in your face!"

Talk about someone ignoring etiquette, or worse yet, slamming a door on someone's toe!

You see, according to Isaiah's prophecy, when the Messiah comes, he will have a heart for the poor, the oppressed, the needy, the hungry, the overlooked ones. The Messiah won't let injustice stand, so wherever there is wrong being committed, the Messiah will make it right. Whenever there is a person being abused, that abuse must stop, and wherever there is poverty and brokenness, the Messiah will step in and reverse that curse.

So, just as Wimber suggests in the quote above, Jesus of Nazareth didn't see his ministry to the poor and oppressed as a moonlighting job on the side. To the Master, it was the primary job description given him by his Father. When the Messiah comes, you see, all oppression and injustice must stop. When God's kingdom comes, the season (or year) of the Lord's merciful grace and favor is extended to all. No-holds-barred. No exceptions. No ifs, buts, or ands.

Now, that's good news, don't you think?

PRAYER

God, I see in Jesus' ministry that demonstrating your loving heart toward the poor, the hungry, the blind, and the oppressed is Job One. I confess that it's easy to delegate your ministry to the poor and needy to lower levels of importance, placing other causes above your insatiable hunger for justice in human affairs. Holy Spirit, may Jesus' primary cause become ours as well. For your name's sake. Amen!

QUESTIONS FOR YOU TO PONDER

- How am I ignoring the fact that Jesus placed his ministry to the oppressed and the outcast at the center of all he does?
- What needs to change in our ministry priorities so that our work for Christ aligns itself more closely with the Luke 4:18-19 messianic commission?

So, what is God speaking to you today as you ponder the *Wisdom of Wimber?*

For too long, many of us have expected government to take care of all the poor and disenfranchised. We are capable of much more in the way of practical aid to these people dear to the heart of God. For example, several years ago our fellowship in conjunction with a county mission refurbished 38 homes of the poor and handicapped in a program called, "Operation Love". We donated time, labor and materials to significantly improve these dwellings. In addition, God has led us to give significant portions of our financial resources to aid the poor in the community and abroad. We are still novices in the ministry to the poor, but we are learning to obey God when he gives us direction in this ministry.[45]

I n Matthew 25:40, Jesus, the King says clearly, "Truly I tell you, whatever you did for one of the least of these brothers and sisters of mine, you did for me."

In this crazy world we live in, both prosperity and poverty are growing rapidly across North America at the same time! As the old saying goes, the rich seem to be getting richer while the poor seem to be getting poorer. Some say the middle class is soon to become a vanishing species. All the while, most Americans believe that it's the government's responsibility to make sure no one falls between the cracks. Yet, if we look carefully at big government's ability to care with great compassion for the individual in need, the track record is pretty scary.

And today, as our national debt in the USA grows by $2.37 billion each day,[46] many wonder if the assistance so many need to survive can continue to be counted upon from Uncle Sam's cash cow that seemed to run dry several decades ago.

Wimber was right when he suggested in 1985 that the church might do a much better job than the government at caring for the poor and needy, if we'd only get off our duffs and just do it. But the question remains today. Will we?

Let me share a few frightening statistics from an article about a book entitled *Passing the Plate: Why Americans Don't Give Away More Money.*[47]

"More than one out of four (over 25%) American Protestants give away no money at all—not even a token $5 per year."

"Of all Christian groups, evangelical Protestants score best (when it comes to giving): only 10 percent give nothing away. Evangelicals tend to be the most generous, but they do not outperform their peers enough to wear a badge of honor. Thirty-six percent report that they give away less than two percent of their income. Only about 27 percent tithe (10% of income)."

"American Christians' lack of generosity might not be as shocking if it didn't contrast so starkly with their astounding wealth. Committed American Christians—those who say their faith is very important to them and those who attend church at least twice a month—earn more than $2.5 trillion dollars every year. On their own, these Christians could be admitted to the G7, the group of the world's seven largest economies! If these Christians gave away 10 percent of their after-tax earnings, they would add another $46 billion to ministry around the world."[48]

Just think of it. 46 billion added dollars to the ministry budgets of churches across America. Imagine how much good work could be done in the name of Jesus if those additional monies were available to assist the poor and needy in our communities? Forty-six billion dollars equally divided amongst the approximately 300,000 Protestant churches across America would add $153,000 to each church's annual budget. And for over ninety percent of American churches, that number represents about a one hundred percent increase in annual giving!

But before you get too excited, let's be gut honest here.

Sadly, if most of our churches were given an additional $153,000 to add to their annual budgets, the track record shows that most pastors and church boards would use up that money on what I referenced earlier: the 3-Bs. My guess is that a typical 3-B pastor would suggest to his or her board that the church spend their cash windfall by 1) improving their (B)uilding; 2) burning (B)ucks on more in-house pet projects; and/or 3) advertising to get more (B)utts in the seats on Sunday morning.

Call me cynical, but something tells me that most of us American pastors would place ministry to the poor way down on our *to do* lists when given $153,000 to spend. Gosh, I'd really like to be proven wrong here, folks, but unless God changes our attitudes toward defining "success" in our churches, we'll keep on keepin' on hoping the government will meet the needs of the poor while the rich get richer and the...well, you know how this saying goes.

Time for a change? I'm guessin' the time has never been better, don't you?

PRAYER

God, it doesn't take a rocket scientist to see how much work needs to be done in meeting the growing needs of the poor in our communities. Spirit, open our eyes to the work that awaits us, and empower us boldly to make the necessary changes in ministry so that your care for the needy is accomplished. For your name's sake. Amen!

QUESTIONS FOR YOU TO PONDER

- What changes need to be made in both our giving attitudes and our church budgets so that we are adequately addressing the great needs of the poor in our communities?
- What outreaches to the poor can become ministries that multiple churches in our city can work on together?

So, what is God speaking to you today as you ponder the *Wisdom of Wimber*?

SALVATION OR SOZO? WHICH WILL IT BE?

Since the late 1940's the American church has been much concerned with saving the lost. For several decades the church has thrown its resources behind massive "Evangelistic Crusades." While many thousands have found Christ in these crusades, the church has fallen short in many cases of making disciples of those who have made decisions. As a religious community the church has naively expected the lost to "come to Church" to be saved. To correct our mistakes we can follow Jesus' example in evangelism. Jesus met the lost and ministered to them on their "turf" even though religious people criticized him for it. After an encounter with Jesus in their own environment, the lost not only made a decision to accept Jesus as Messiah, they became true disciples whose lives were radically altered by the power and love of God. In the Body of Christ it is each person's role to minister salvation to the lost. Often we think of "saving souls," but salvation is for the "whole man." Often the poor, the lost, and the sick are the same people.[49]

As a baby-boomer, I grew up being very familiar with evangelistic crusades. I credit the great evangelist, Billy Graham, as the man who clearly brought me to the salvation message of Jesus Christ. While I grew up in church, faithfully attending a main-line denominational church with my parents, it was actually Billy Graham's evangelistic crusades on television that convinced me to make a personal decision to follow Jesus.

Back in the day, you see, Billy Graham was on TV regularly. Most of his large crusades in the 1950s and 60s were broadcast across the airwaves, and with only three major TV networks available to us back then, it wouldn't be unusual to turn on the tube on any given evening and find Billy preaching to yet another massive crowd in some major American city. My parents enjoyed watching Billy and I

141

did as well. I often tell people that I responded to Billy's invitation to "come, just as you are" many, many times on TV, and for all I know, it stuck at least one time; maybe more!

Yet, while massive evangelistic crusades were very effective during the second half of the twentieth century across North America, Wimber is right when he said that sadly, most of evangelical Christianity views the word *salvation* as being associated exclusively with sinners receiving Christ as Savior, much as I did when I was a kid.

But here's the truth.

When you and I limit the use of the word salvation to such evangelistic activity, we miss the fact that the New Testament has a much broader theme in mind when the word appears. In fact, the New Testament Greek word for salvation is sozo and it means so much more than some sinner saying a prayer of dedication at an evangelistic crusade. If we take a quick peek into a New Testament Greek Lexicon, we'll find these extensive definitions of the word SOZO (salvation or being saved):

- To save, keep safe and sound, to rescue from danger or destruction;
- To save one from injury or peril;
- To save a suffering one from perishing, i.e., one suffering from disease;
- To make well, heal, restore to health;
- To preserve one who is in danger of destruction, to save or rescue;
- To deliver from the penalties of the messianic judgment;
- To save from the evils, which obstruct the reception of the messianic deliverance.

Now don't get me wrong. I'm not saying that we should stop encouraging people to get saved by praying the sinner's prayer, but what I believe Wimber thought needed to change in American church life was our very limited view of what *salvation* (sozo) should actually be. You see, to John Wimber, *sozo* also included the extensive ministries of Jesus' healing and deliverance power. *Sozo* also includes Jesus' ministry of compassion to the poor, the oppressed, and the needy.

So when Wimber talked about taking *salvation* to the streets, he literally meant taking the full gospel of Jesus on the road. The good news that includes not only a concise message of salvation to the lost, but also the compassionate works of Jesus, including healing of the sick, casting out demons, feeding the hungry, clothing the naked, and offering to meet the practical needs of people as well as their spiritual needs.

As I see it, it might do the American church of the twenty-first century well to remember this broader definition of *salvation* as well. In a time when the credibility of the church is being questioned more and more, it might do great wonders for our Christian witness if we did a bit less hard-core *salvation* preaching to the sinners and a whole bunch more demonstrations of *sozo* to the masses. As Wimber would so often point out, it's so much easier to talk to a person about receiving Jesus as Savior after you've just filled their family's empty stomachs, or healed a family member of a life-threatening sickness!

Prayer

Father God, I'm afraid that my generation has taken Jesus' magnificent ministry of sozo and reduced it down to just getting a sinner to pray a short prayer of salvation. May your Holy Spirit forgive us for such actions and allow the church to once again expand the amazing ministry of Jesus' sozo power to the whole person. For your name's sake. Amen!

Questions for You to Ponder

- What might it look like for Christian ministries today to expand the base of what *salvation* actually means?
- What will it take to transform our Christian outreaches from simply preaching a "turn-or-burn" salvation message into a much broader compassion ministry that focuses on healing the sick, casting out darkness, caring for the poor, the needy, and the oppressed, while still proclaiming the Good News salvation message of Jesus to all?

So, what is God speaking to you today as you ponder the *Wisdom of Wimber?*

We conceive in our philosophy, leadership not as a position, a title, power, authority, respect, or privilege…but as an obligation to service and self-sacrifice.

I'm not talking about false humility and putting yourself down. I'm talking about a willingness to render unassuming service.

That's what Jesus called for in Luke 17 when he told the story of the servant who went out into the field and came in that night. All he had done at the end of the day was to render humble service. All any of us will have done by the end of the day is render humble service. It doesn't matter whether you have to plow five hundred acres or one that day, you've just rendered humble service. You're the Master's and the Master can employ you any way he desires.

I don't care if you are recruiting a drummer, an usher, or a nursery worker…if he or she doesn't understand that we humbly render our service *to the Lord*, then they'll constantly look for rewards.[50]

Sadly, so many Christians say they have a heart for the poor and needy, but then when asked to help directly with a "hands-on" ministry effort, they reply, "Sorry, no. That's why I give my money to the church, so the church can do it."

On many occasions, parishioners at Wimber's church would come up to him with ministry suggestions. "Pastor, I know a family in my neighborhood who needs some help with their finances. Can the church do something to help them?" John would chuckle and then say, "Yes, I agree. I believe the church should indeed help those neighbors of yours. You have my full permission to go help them with their needs!"

As I see it, the compassion ministry of Jesus is for everybody. In truth, the only ministry Jesus has is the ministry of compassion. As we discussed in the last section above, the New Testament Greek word *sozo* envelopes the entirety of Jesus mission here on earth.

Thus, when Jesus commissioned his friends to go and make disciples across the world, teaching them to do and say everything he taught them (see Matthew 28), he was basically giving us all his ministry of *sozo*. Around our Vineyard church in Cedar Rapids, we call it Jesus' mission to go and love "the hell" out of everyone and anyone we come in contact with!

From Wimber's perspective, there was no distinction between those in full-time pastoral ministry and those who sat in the pews on Sunday morning. When it came to ministering God's love to the poor, the wounded, the hungry, and the oppressed; everybody needs to play and no one is excluded from the call.

Simple, humble service unto the Lord then became Wimber's mission in life. He often told us of the way he thought of himself as a coin in the Lord's pocket saying, "Spend me, Jesus, the way you'd like to spend me, today." To Wimber, he didn't care, quite honestly, if the Master placed him in front of thousands or in front of just one or two. For him, the job of serving Jesus faithfully was all the same; or as one pastor said it, "When working for Jesus, the pay is the same!"

So, as we come to this conclusion on the subject of compassion, let's agree together that from now on, we'll no longer set aside certain individuals in our midst as those who care for the poor or the hungry. When it comes to caring for the less fortunate, let's determine up front that all of us in the community of Christ are called, commissioned, and empowered by the Spirit to throw ourselves headlong into the *sozo* ministry of Jesus. And with his hands and heart leading the way, amazing things can happen as we care for souls, one person at a time, in the compassion ministries of our Master.

PRAYER

Jesus, your commission is quite clear. Your entire church is called, commissioned, and sent out in your name to say and do all the things you said and did two thousand years ago. Without wavering, I choose to say "yes" to my part of your Great Commission. Give me your heart, your compassion, your strength, and your love, so that I might go, being your hands to the broken and needy ones. For your name's sake. Amen!

QUESTIONS FOR YOU TO PONDER

- Rather than waiting for others to care for the poor and meet the needs of the oppressed, what specific actions can I take today to enter into Jesus' *sozo* ministry?
- Where, in my city, is there a great need? Where, in my neighborhood, can I begin today to bring the compassion of Jesus to those in great need?

So, what is God speaking to you today as you ponder the *Wisdom of Wimber?*

You're the Master's and the Master can

employ you any way he desires.

On Healing

My job (is) to obey, pray, and rely on his sovereign mercy;

his part (is) to heal.

Praying for the Sick

In Matthew 28: 18-20, the great commission passage, Jesus told the disciples to "go and make disciples of all nations...*teaching them to obey everything I have commanded you.*" They were to carry out his ministry, which included praying for the sick.[51]

My job (is) to obey, pray, and rely on his sovereign mercy; his part (is) to heal.[52]

As I see it, church historians may one day look back at the life and ministry of Wimber and find that one of the greatest gifts he gave the church-at-large was both the permission and the encouragement for the common man or woman sitting in the pew to get up out of their seat and follow Jesus into his healing ministry.

In all honesty, before Wimber began equipping the saints to pray for the sick back in the early 1980s, the healing ministry of Jesus was pretty much either 1) ignored completely by most churches; or 2) reserved for those "special people" who believed themselves to be uniquely anointed by the Holy Spirit to pray for the sick.

Indeed, when it came to joining Jesus in his healing ministry, for Wimber, not only could everybody play, but everybody is commissioned by Jesus to pray! So back in the day, when our church in Evanston, Illinois, first came across Wimber, it was mighty scary to know that he expected all of us to begin praying for the sick. In fact, the first time I attended a Wimber conference in 1985, I was shocked to see him inviting a bunch of young kids to the front of the auditorium so they could learn to pray for people who had come up for healing! In fact, before that first conference was over, I was equally shocked to find myself praying for others, asking God to heal them of diseases I couldn't even pronounce!

You see, for Wimber, praying for the sick was part-and-parcel with following Jesus. Thus, healing wasn't a special power given to anointed people, but a kingdom ministry accomplished by Jesus as we simply do our part. We obey Jesus by praying with those who are sick. He does what only he can do: heal and impart his presence as we pray.

In the process, literally thousands of pew-sitters were given both permission and the encouragement to become pro-active in the healing ministry of Jesus. And while healing can never be subjugated into a formula, John also gave us two handy tools that helped all of us as we took these brave new steps into an arena most of us thought needed to be left to the professionals. The first tool was a set of biblically based principles that set the stage for us as we began praying for the sick. John called this tool a set of six healing concepts. Here's the list:

Six Healing Concepts

1. God wants to heal the sick today.
2. God is looking for a corporate ministry of healing.
3. Our trust in God is demonstrated by our actions.
4. We must be empowered by and led by the Holy Spirit.
5. Importance of loving relationships with our brothers & sisters.
6. God wants to heal the whole person, not just the specific condition.

Quite honestly, these six concepts, when acted upon, took our straight-laced, evangelical church body and turned it into a community of every-day Christians who truly believed that Jesus would heal the sick in our midst if all of us would simply do our part and pray.

Second, he gave us a valuable five-step prayer model that became, not a formula for healing, but an easily followed set of reminders for those who truly believed that Jesus was looking for his followers to pray faithfully for healing. In our next few sections, we'll unpack John's five-step healing model and review each step, one by one.

WIMBER'S 5-STEP HEALING MODEL

1. **The Interview**: Where does it hurt?
2. **The Diagnostic Decision**: What is the Father saying?
3. **The Prayer Selection**: What kind of prayer is needed to help this person?
4. **The Prayer Engagement**: How effective are our prayers?
5. **The Post-Prayer Direction**: What's next?

PRAYER

Father, I thank you for the amazing impact Wimber had in my life; opening the door for me into Jesus' healing ministry, encouraging me that I could participate if I simply did my part to pray for the sick. Now Lord, all these years later, I'm so glad John taught me these biblical truths and indeed, Father, I've seen you work amazing healing into so many lives. For your name's sake. Amen!

QUESTIONS FOR YOU TO PONDER

- What reservations keep me from acting on the six biblically based principles of healing that John Wimber taught about?
- Am I leaving the ministry of healing to others?
- And if so, why am I doing that?
- What needs to change in my life so that I'm fully participating with Jesus as he continues his healing ministry across the world today?

So, what is God speaking to you today as you ponder the *Wisdom of Wimber*?

THE INTERVIEW: WHERE DOES IT HURT?

The first step in healing prayer is the interview. *The interview answers the question, "Where does it hurt?"* I ask, "What do you want me to pray for?" Then I listen to the answer on two levels: the natural and the supernatural. On a natural level I evaluate the answer in light of my biblical knowledge, what I know about the person, and my past experience in praying for similar problems in other people. This is not a medical interview in which we probe for a technical, medical history. A medical history is important for medical treatments, but not for praying for people's healing. The Holy Spirit is the doctor and the cure; he does not need our technical knowledge to heal. Besides, detailed medical discussions usually only delay healing prayer.[53]

W hen Wimber taught us his five-step healing model (see previous section), some criticized him for attempting to formularize something that can only be categorized as one of the mysteries of God. Supernatural healing from above, you see, is never systematic; nor is it ever predictable. Wimber would always be quick to remind us that praying successfully for the sick was never something we humans could completely understand, nor could we ever hope to contain or manipulate healing in such a way that it would make this amazing ministry within the kingdom manageable.

But while John never expected the ministry of healing to become manageable or predictable, he did do us all a favor by giving us his set of guidelines, which Wimber believed, could be readily substantiated with examples taken directly from Jesus' healing ministry itself.

We begin with the first step, the interview. This step sets the stage for everything else that happens when praying for the sick. As you can see from Wimber's quote above, he believed that there were several components to the interview. I believe that within those components, when done with great care, an environment where healing can occur can truly be encouraged.

Sadly, in many churches where the healing ministry of Jesus is practiced, the whole process of praying for the sick takes on a highly religious tone. Often, the leader who is praying for the sick, stands on the stage, and with microphone in hand, tells a person in the crowd what's wrong with them. Next, the leader invokes a short, stern prayer for healing and, then, most often, commands the person to sit down and believe that he or she is healed.

Yikes.

Now don't get me wrong, I've seen God work powerfully with such a process, but quite honestly, I believe the Master never healed people with this model. As I see it, Jesus' powerful ministry of healing for people was always birthed out of his great love and compassion for those who needed a touch from God. So often, we in leadership forget what the ancient church called "the cure (or care) of souls."[54] You see, each person Jesus healed was treated, not like a project, but as a person. So when Wimber taught us to always begin our healing prayer with an interview, he was reminding us that there is a great need for the people we pray for to be treated compassionately and with tender hands and a warm heart.

Too often, I've found myself, and others, treating healing as a powerful tool of ministry that I do in Jesus' name instead of an act of mercy and compassion that Jesus wants it to be. So when Wimber suggested we begin with an interview, we are taking the extra time we so often forget to do, in treating the person with great respect and love. Making sure a person is relaxed and comfortable is so important to the healing process. And while we're asking questions of the one who is looking for healing, we're also slowing ourselves down, listening to the Lord for what he sees rather than quickly acting out of our presuppositions of what we might believe the person's problem is.

I am thankful that Wimber reminded us to take the extra time to treat people as Jesus always did. Never do I see Jesus commanding loud, boisterous prayers for healing over a crowd of people. Never do I see Jesus ram-rodding his way through a prayer so he can move on to the next person in line. And never do I see Jesus insisting that the person he's praying for name-it-or-claim-it to be healed. But what I do see is Jesus treating people with great compassion and loving care, like a caring shepherd, leading his wounded flock to pools of living water.

PRAYER

Jesus, thank you for reminding me through Wimber's model that it's vitally important for me to always treat those I'm praying for as people and not projects. I readily confess that it's easy to take your ministry of healing and make it into a power trip where others look to me as the "healer." I choose to lay that ugly stuff down, Lord, and ask that you always remind me to start any time of healing prayer with a simple, relaxing interview where the person I'm praying for feels relaxed and comfortable in your presence. For your name's sake. Amen!

QUESTIONS FOR YOU TO PONDER

- What might it look like in my church setting to slow down the fast-paced ministries we do, so that people in our midst are treated as people and not projects?
- Where am I overlooking the ancient art of the "cure (or care) of souls," where taking extra time with an individual person trumps my drive to get big projects completed?

So, what is God speaking to you today as you ponder the *Wisdom of Wimber*?

THE DIAGNOSIS: WHAT IS THE FATHER SAYING?

The second step in the healing procedure is making a diagnostic decision, that is, identifying and clarifying the root of the person's problem. *The diagnostic decision answers the question, "Why does this person have this condition?"* This is a crucial step in the healing procedure, because it determines the type of prayer needed to bring healing.

In fact, this procedure overlaps with the first step (the interview). While I am interviewing the person, on a supernatural level I ask God for insight into the ultimate cause of the condition. These insights usually come to me through words of knowledge, words of wisdom, and distinguishing of spirits.

The Holy Spirit is the one who leads us through the diagnostic step. He walks with us, accompanying us through the process. (And) in the end, the burden for healing is on him, not us.[55]

I n truth, most of the church-at-large in our Western society looks at physical healing as something that should be left to the doctors.

Now don't get me wrong. Wimber thoroughly believed in the great blessings of healing that can come through the hands of modern medicine. But he also believed that Jesus of Nazareth still has a healing ministry and that ministry is still accessible to those who are willing to step into it, learning from the Master along the way.

In the earliest days of the Vineyard movement, John and Carol Wimber were invited by the Lord to explore the ancient art of healing as practiced by Jesus and his disciples in the first century. Yet, for most of Wimber's life prior to the Lord's invitation, he saw supernatural healing as something to be avoided. In his testimony, *I'm a Fool for Christ, Whose Fool are You?*, he states clearly that before the Holy Spirit invited him to explore the healing ministry of Jesus, as described in the New Testament, healing in church settings was something he readily associated with charlatanry and swindlers.

But all that changed as he began exploring how Jesus taught his disciples to pray for the sick. In truth, Wimber's 5-step healing model (see previous section) was developed as Wimber unpacked the countless healing stories found throughout the New Testament.

Step two in this model, the diagnostic decision, came as a direct revelation from the Holy Spirit as John was reflecting on the healing stories found in the gospels. There, on so many occasions, we find Jesus ministering to people in ways that seem inconsistent to the way our human intellect operates.

Take, for example, the lame man who was brought to Jesus by his friends (Mark 2:1-12). After working their way through the crowd, this man's friends cut open the roof of the building Jesus was ministering in and lowered their friend down on ropes so that he might be touched and healed by Jesus. It's apparent from Mark's gospel that everyone expected Jesus to pray for the lame man, healing him so that he might walk again. But Jesus surprises and even shocks the crowd by saying to the lame man, "Son, your sins are forgiven."

This statement caused the religious leaders in the crowd to push back at Jesus, declaring that only God can speak words of forgiveness over people. Most pastors take this text and preach about how Jesus, as God's Son, did have the full right to speak forgiveness over the lame man. And while that truth is evident in this story, Wimber took this text even further and saw, in this same story, a prime example where Jesus is apparently listening to the Father at the same time the lame man and his friends are looking specifically to Jesus for physical healing.

In John 5, Jesus declares to his friends that he only did what he saw the Father doing. And in this case of the lame man (in Mark 2) who was looking for physical healing, could it be that the Father was whispering into Jesus' ear that this man's healing was somehow connected to a sinful condition? While the text doesn't reveal an answer for us, I find it intriguing that rather than going into a prayer for physical healing, Jesus takes the conversation in a completely different direction. Rather than addressing the physical ailment of this lame man, Jesus directs his comments (through the prompting of the Father?) onto issues of sin.

As John Wimber suggests, when you and I are praying for the sick, it's vitally important for us to be listening to both the person we are preparing to pray for *and* to the Holy Spirit at the same time! I've found, over the years, that if I truly listen carefully, the Spirit does, very often, give me indications of how to direct my prayers, as I begin to pray.

I recall one incident when my wife and I were preparing to pray for a woman who was asking God to open her womb so that she and her husband might have a child. They had been childless for years and all of their attempts to get pregnant, even with the help of medical assistance, had proved fruitless. As we were listening to her story, both Sandy and I got a sense from the Lord that we were to not immediately pray for her request to get pregnant, but were to ask her a bit about some painful experiences she had in the past. Thank God, one thing led to another, and after a powerful time of prayer, breaking off old wounds of unforgiveness, we finally prayed for her to become pregnant. A few weeks later, she came back and told us that God had finally answered their prayers. They were pregnant!

That story confirmed for us, once again, that Wimber's suggestion to listen carefully for the Father's diagnosis before entering into our prayers does truly play a major role in the way you and I should pray for those who are seeking healing from above.

PRAYER

Thank you, Jesus, for explaining to us how you operated in your ministry. If you intentionally chose to wait for the Father to show you what to say and do, how much more must I be willing to do that same thing? Holy Spirit, give me both a patience to wait and an ear to hear, as I learn the fine art of healing. For your name's sake. Amen!

QUESTIONS FOR YOU TO PONDER

- How often do I assume that I know what to pray for without ever waiting for God to give me his direction or guidance on how to pray?
- What practical steps can I take in slowing down my actions so, like Jesus, I will find myself doing and saying only those things I sense the Father asking of me to say and do?

So, what is God speaking to you today as you ponder the *Wisdom of Wimber?*

The Prayer Selection: Prayers, Prayers, and More Prayers

The third step of the healing procedure is prayer selection. *This step answers the question, "What kind of prayer is needed to help this person?"*

There are many ways in which we may pray for healing…several different kinds of prayers used in divine healing – prayers of petition and intercession, words of command, and so on. These different types of healing prayers fall into two categories, petitions directed toward God and words that we receive from God and speak to a condition or demon.[56]

Not until I met Wimber, did I realize that we have so many different healing prayers to choose from when we pray for the sick! And much like Wimber's testimony, it wasn't until I actually took the time to scour the New Testament for myself, looking specifically at Jesus' prayers for healing, did I begin to move away from my longtime, one-and-only prayer for healing, "God, guide the surgeon's hand!" I now have a toolbox of different prayers available to me when I pray for those who are looking to Jesus for healing.

Let's start, first and foremost, with the type of prayers that you and I are most familiar with. Many people call these prayers of petition or intercessory prayer. I like to call them God-directed prayers.

My long-time standard, "Guide the doctor's hand," is a prayer of petition, and while this prayer is not a bad one, I must confess that for most of my life prior to meeting Wimber, I used this prayer in a way that was conveying to God more resignation on my part than anything else. But something changed for me when I began to study the prayers of Jesus. It was then I started to see the real power behind his prayers of petition.

Take the Lord's Prayer, for example. When Jesus prays, "your kingdom come, your will be done," this is a prayer of petition where Jesus is going much further than making a mere suggestion to God. Jesus is actually invoking the in-breaking powers of God's kingdom, asking God, his Father, to step into this immediate moment, bringing with him his sovereign right to make earthly situations conform to the sovereignty of God Almighty.

These prayers of petition and invocation are so much more than just a feeble hope. While invoking God's presence might seem a bit bold to some, quite honestly, it's always important when praying for others to remind ourselves that we truly need God's presence if anything of any importance is going to happen. Prayers such as "Come, Holy Spirit" or "Jesus, we ask you to be with us here right now" might seem strange to some, but over the years, I've found that it is always good to remind ourselves that our prayers for the sick will fall worthless to the ground unless Jesus and his healing presence is there. As Psalm 127:1 says so succinctly, "Unless the Lord builds the house, those who labor, do so in vain." Prayers of petition when prayed in firm belief of God's powerful sovereignty, do bring his power and presence in ways that are quite amazing!

The second type of prayer Wimber taught us to pray is somewhat different than a God-directed prayer of petition. As I see it, these prayers are the kind that most of us are not very comfortable praying! Yet when one studies the prayers of Jesus, we will begin to see him using, what some call, a commanding prayer, or a proclamation prayer. This is the type of prayer where Jesus isn't asking God for healing (petition), but Jesus, himself, is proclaiming a truth or command directly to the person he is praying for, or even more interesting, to what we, in our Westernized society, would consider as an inanimate object.

Often in the gospels, we find Jesus, when he is ministering to a sick person, speaking directly to that person, ("Be healed," "See" or "Take up your mat and walk"). And on other occasions, we find Jesus speaking directly to a disease or a demon, commanding these objects to move away from the person who is being afflicted or tormented by them.

Now, to be quite honest, learning to pray these types of proclamation prayers over others is difficult, at best. But as Wimber suggests, there will be times as you and I pray for the sick, when we will feel an unction or inward push from God's Spirit to speak out with authority a strong prayer of proclamation or command. It's been my personal experience that these types of prayers are not ones that originate in my mind, but seem to be born out of a powerful unction of God's Spirit, given in his authority to speak God's will into a situation where less than that has been occurring.

PRAYER

Jesus, I stand amazed at your model for healing found in the gospels. Indeed, you had a tool-belt of different prayers that you used wisely in each situation that came your way. Holy Spirit, teach me, empower me, and in-dwell me as I go out and pray for the sick. May I learn, along the way, the many tools of prayer readily available to me. For your name's sake. Amen!

QUESTIONS FOR YOU TO PONDER

- What changes do I need to make in my approach to the healing ministry of Jesus?
- Am I utilizing the full array of prayers modeled for me by Jesus, or am I using a "one-size-fits-all" prayer of petition approach?
- What additional prayers, like proclamation prayers, or prayers of command, can I add to my healing tool-belt?

So, what is God speaking to you today as you ponder the *Wisdom of Wimber?*

The Prayer Engagement: How Effective Are Our Prayers?

The fourth step of the healing procedure is prayer engagement. *This step answers the question, "How effective are our prayers?"* The prayer engagement consists of prayer, laying on of hands, and, when needed, further interviewing. The way we pray is determined by our diagnostic decision and prayer selection.

After laying on hands, I pray aloud that the Holy Spirit come and minister to the person. My prayers are quite simple: "Holy Spirit, I invite you to come on this person and release your healing power," or "Holy Spirit, come and show us how to pray," or, more succinctly, "Holy Spirit, come."

People respond to the power of the Holy Spirit in ways that are not always predictable. These "manifestations," or phenomena that occur among people in response to God's power and truth, vary in form: falling over, shaking, sobbing, laughing, screaming out – the list of unusual emotional and physical phenomena is quite long.[57]

As you can see from reading Wimber's quote above, the actual prayer engagement, when using his model, is vastly different than the typical approach to prayer taught in most churches. In the past, I'd always been taught to fold my hands and close my eyes when I prayed. But Wimber taught us a radically different approach. And as I see it, the idea of keeping my eyes open as I pray for someone, looking and listening for what God might be doing while asking questions of the person I'm praying for, is a difficult change for many, but well worth the effort when we do!

Over the years, as I've prayed for the sick, it's amazing to see how many times God steps in and begins to work as I cooperate with his time table. Rather than quickly blurting out a nice little healing prayer, I've learned that waiting and watching as I pray pays great dividends in the process. Many times, for example, people who are being prayed for do receive from Jesus if we can just relax and let that happen.

I recall one recent prayer experience when I was praying for a person, and after a longer period of silence, I noticed their countenance changing. When we began the prayer for healing, the person seemed rather frustrated and wound-up. But several minutes later as we slowed it down and I encouraged the person to relax, I noticed that the person became much more peaceful. Taking Wimber's advice, I quietly asked the person what they were feeling. The person hesitated at first to talk, but I reminded them that our conversation wouldn't interrupt Jesus' work, so the person said, "I feel more peace inside." We waited for a while longer, and then I asked again, "What's going on now?" The person responded that they felt warmth over their head and shoulders. In this particular case, the Lord obviously wanted to heal the person's anxiousness and worry about their ailment. As it turned out, the person went home that evening and reported a breakthrough with their sickness the next day!

Thanks to this simple prayer model, I was able to use some of the ideas that I learned, while slowing down my prayer engagement with that person, thus giving the Lord much more time and space to do what he wanted to do. Looking back at that particular prayer time, I realized that I actually prayed few words but asked a lot more questions. In the process, Jesus took his time to touch the person in deeper places than I could ever access.

Thanks, John, for sharing this model!

Next, let's look at Wimber's fifth and final step: The Post-Prayer Direction.

PRAYER

Jesus, on one hand, it's amazing to me that you invite me to join you in your healing ministry. Yet, thanks to your servant, John Wimber, I've come to realize that you really do enjoy working with me as I'm praying for healing with others. Holy Spirit, may I always give you plenty of time to work as I'm praying my prayers for healing. For your name's sake. Amen!

QUESTIONS FOR YOU TO PONDER

- In our fast-paced world where 'git-r-done' is both the procedure and the process, how can I slow myself down long enough to allow the Lord to engage with a person as I'm praying for their healing?
- What needs to change in my prayers for others so that they know it's both permissible and positive to take our time, interacting with both God and with each other as we're seeking healing from above?

So what is God speaking to you today as you ponder the *Wisdom of Wimber*?

THE POST-PRAYER DIRECTION: WHAT'S NEXT?

The last step in the healing procedure is the post-prayer directions. *The post-prayer directions answer the questions, "What should this person do to remain healed?" and "What should this person do if he or she was not healed?"* When people are not healed I reassure them that God loves them and encourage them to seek more prayer. Usually that means directing them to a prayer team or kinship group in which they may receive longer-term prayer.

I instruct those who are healed to sin no more and no longer follow the ways of the flesh (see John 8:11). This involves a variety of practical advice, determined by the problem, that includes advice about the Scripture reading and study, prayer, and works of righteousness. The key to maintaining these spiritual disciplines and living free of sin, though, is living within the context of overall pastoral care.[58]

Back in the day, when John and Carol Wimber gave us their 5-step healing model, I'm sure that they would never have dreamed that those of us who took their model and ran with it, would forget that the healing of the sick is not a ministry project to pursue, but part-and-parcel with Jesus' mission of compassion to a broken world.

You see, over the years, I've found that it's really easy to take Wimber's 5-step healing model and allow it to evolve into yet another systematic approach to "doing ministry" in our Americanized churches, where getting the job done is more important than the actual care of individual souls.

It is still very possible and maybe even likely that you and I will begin to approach this model in some sterile, "git-r-done" way where we are more interested in following the steps than we are the actual care of the person we're praying for.

So, as I see it, that's why Wimber included this fifth and maybe the most important step, in this model.

For Wimber, healing of the sick was seen as a ministry that Jesus gave to his entire church, not just to individuals. Praying for the sick was something the Wimbers envisioned for everyone in a church to be doing. Not just the pastor, nor the anointed leaders; but everyone and anyone, on any given Sunday morning and throughout the week, could pray for healing for others. And in truth, it is in this context of true Christian community where real healing can occur!

Thus, when someone receives prayer for healing from us, it's vital that we place that prayer for healing in the full context of the life of the church. If healing is really going to work, it's vital that the person being prayed for is encouraged to seek out on-going relationship with both the Lord (the originator of the healing itself!) and a community of believers where love and encouragement is available on a continuing basis. Healing, you see, in Jesus' kingdom economy, is never a project unto itself, but an invitation to relationship. It is a relationship with the Master and with a group of dedicated Christ-followers.

So often, for example, I've seen folks we've prayed for receive a certain amount of healing as we've prayed for them; but after the prayer, those same people go home, making little or no long-term changes in their basic approach to life, and sadly, the healing touch they seemed to receive fades away into the sunset.

Let me use this example.

I recall praying quite regularly with a man in our church for healing of his sexual addictions. Each time we prayed, he would receive a nice touch of healing from the Lord. Yet despite our advice (post-prayer direction) to plug himself into a small group of men where he could become more involved with a community of guys who would love and support him, he continued to be a loner, never taking the necessary steps to involve himself more openly with those who would care for him. As a result, his addictions were never really healed and over time, he gradually pulled away from the church, and to this day, I know he has never really allowed God to touch his deepest wounds where true healing is needed.

Now please, don't misunderstand. I'm not saying that a person will lose their healing if they fail to make radical changes in their lives. Post-prayer direction must be done in a sensitive and caring manner. There's nothing worse than being preached at by a bunch of well-meaning, judgmental Christians immediately following a sweet time of prayer with Jesus. But it is vitally important that each prayer session for healing be concluded with a "what's next" type of discussion. It's this care of the whole person that sets Wimber's model head-n-shoulders above others that simply encourage people to pray for the sick and then walk away, hoping the person can make it on their own.

PRAYER

Father, thank you for the completeness I see in John's 5-step healing model. May I never treat healing as a project to be done, but as an extension of your merciful, long-lasting love and care for your people. May the healing ministry of Jesus be released once again into the context of your community of saints. For your name's sake. Amen!

QUESTIONS FOR YOU TO PONDER

- What might it look like for the community of believers I'm a part of to step fully into the healing ministry of Jesus?
- What could it look like if everyone in my church were participating with Jesus in healing rather than assigning it to just a few?
- Finally, what variety of support ministries might be needed as follow-up to our healing prayers for others so that our post-prayer direction has practical application?

So, what is God speaking to you today as you ponder the *Wisdom of Wimber*?

When people are not healed I reassure them that God loves them and encourage them to seek more prayer.

On Mission

Jesus proclaimed and demonstrated God's right to rule creation

as he destroyed the works of Satan (1 Jn. 3:8)

Doing an Ancient Thing in a Contemporary Way

When we started (early days of the Vineyard), we did not jump on the bandwagon of "God's new thing." Instead, we set out to do an ancient thing in a contemporary way: train people to continue the kingdom ministry of Jesus. Tired of my ministry, I was desperate to see his.

What exactly is kingdom ministry? Luke gives a glimpse into Jesus' own self perception. At his coronation address he announced his kingly agenda:

"The Spirit of the Lord is on me, because he has anointed me to preach good news to the poor. He has sent me to proclaim freedom for the prisoners and recovery of sight for the blind, to release the oppressed, to proclaim the year of the Lord's favor."

In the gospels we find Jesus' action plan for Spirit-empowered ministry: Jesus

- taught.
- preached good news to the poor and poor in spirit.
- proclaimed freedom to prisoners bound in sin and darkness.
- cast out demons.
- healed the sick.
  and he
- mentored disciples to do the same.

Jesus proclaimed and demonstrated God's right to rule creation as he destroyed the works of Satan (1 Jn. 3:8). He equipped followers and promised that they too would do what he did

173

because "everyone who is fully trained will be like his teacher" (Lk. 6:40, Mt. 28:16-20; Jn. 14:12-14).

I view this process of kingdom ministry as a continuum.[59]

Today, there is so much chatter amongst church leaders about how the church-at-large can best accomplish our mission. Many pastors and church leaders, myself included, have spent countless hours composing complex mission statements, carefully crafting words that will best motivate our parishioners to get up out of the pews and go into our community, fulfilling the mission we believe our church has been given by God.

Sadly, after thirty years of pastoral ministry, I must admit that most of my valiant efforts over the years to write visionary mission statements that will stir people to action have fallen flat on their face. Oh yes, my flowery words might look good on a website or when published in a church newsletter; but quite honestly, most of my efforts to produce a powerful mission-driven purpose statement for my church have produced only a flurry of activity that quickly wears out after a few initial months of excitement. In truth, most of the mission statements I've run across in churches in recent years are little more than nice words full of big-plans that are birthed out of self-centered interests and fleshly ambition to do some good things for God!

As I see it, it's time for me and my church (and maybe yours as well?) to return to the simplicity of mission that John Wimber spoke of years ago. You see, to John, all mission was about doing "an ancient thing in a contemporary way"...following Jesus into his kingdom ministry. And just in case we ever lost track of what Jesus' kingdom ministry looked like, Wimber would always have us open up our Bibles to the fourth chapter of the Gospel of Luke 4.18-19:

The Spirit of the Lord is on me,
    because he has anointed me
    to proclaim good news to the poor.

174

He has sent me to proclaim freedom for the prisoners
and recovery of sight for the blind,
to set the oppressed free,
to proclaim the year of the Lord's favor (NIV).

As we've discussed earlier in this book, Wimber called this section of Scripture (Luke 4: 18-19), "Jesus' job description." If you recall, Jesus spoke these words just as he was starting his ministry in his hometown of Nazareth. And it was Wimber's premise that everything you and I see Jesus doing and saying over the next three years of ministry is activity that is simply fleshing out in detail, all that Jesus had in mind on that fateful day as he announced that this messianic passage from Isaiah 61 was being fulfilled in the hearing of his listeners.

So, kingdom mission is not an add-on to our churches, or an option we throw into the mix like when we buy a new minivan with added perks like power doors, video screens, and seven-passenger seating. According to Wimber, doin' the stuff Jesus speaks about in Luke 4:18-19 is the only option in mission for those who desire to follow the Master wherever he might go.

So how about if you and I toss out our flowery mission statements, take out the trash on our good ministry ideas for Jesus, and get back to the simplicity of mission found in Luke 4: 18-19? In the next few sections, we'll unpack a few more Wimber quotes on the subject of mission. Keep reading and come along for the ride.

PRAYER

Father, it's abundantly clear to me that I've spent a lot of time, energy, and resources trying to develop a powerful mission statement for my church, only to realize that you've already written the book on the subject! Spirit, empower me and indwell me to simplify the mission and return to the clear instructions of Jesus found in Luke's gospel. For your name's sake. Amen!

QUESTIONS FOR YOU TO PONDER

- What might it look like for me and my church to drop all

other missionary ideas and dedicate ourselves completely to fulfilling Luke 4: 18-19 in our community?

- What needs to change in our approach to ministry and mission so that we simplify our efforts and focus exclusively on continuing the kingdom ministry of Jesus in our midst?

So what is God speaking to you today as you ponder the *Wisdom of Wimber*?

Our Primary Mission: Being Kingdom People

Today the buzz word in leadership training is vision. Sometimes I wonder if we have it right. What I do in the Vineyard is ask Jesus to build his vision and strategy among us. I am trying to keep up with him and believe and do what his book says. So what is Jesus' vision? The kingdom of God.

Our primary aim in life is to love and glorify God and expand his kingdom in relevant ways in the time allotted us. As communities of the King, Vineyard churches should model what the kingdom looks like when God has his way with a group of people.[60]

Mission is the word we use to define the work to which Christ calls his followers. While the specifics might vary in different church settings, the church-at-large has understood over the centuries that once a person fully embraces their call to salvation, the commission of Christ is readily available, extended by the Holy Spirit to all, inviting Jesus followers across the globe into the ministry and mission of the Master. Church planting and church growth naturally occur, when the ministry or mission of Jesus is being acted upon. Right?

But before we go further here in talking about mission, let me clear the air about this church growth theme we keep hearing about in so much of the Americanized church today. As I see it, just as vision was the buzz word for leaders back in Wimber's day, church planting and church growth seems to be the key topic for so many pastors across North America today.

Now, please, don't get me wrong.

In truth, the basic principles of church planting and church growth are good. God desires his church to grow, flourish, expand, and reach to the ends of the earth. The Jesus found in the New Testament is not against church growth. Nor are we.

But here's the rub.

After thirty plus years of doing church using the basic principles of church growth, I have to give you, my deep-down, dirty little confession.

If you've been a regular reader of my blog (www.pastorboller. com), you know that God has been working on me in recent years, setting me free from what I call the 3-Bs, where all of my success or failure as a pastor is measured by (B)uilding size, (B)ucks in the offering, and (B)utts in the seats! As God has been stripping away my dependency on the 3-Bs, I must sadly confess to you, my friends, that he has also exposed, underneath it all, an ugly, fleshly personal ambition parading behind much of my church growth attitude over the years.

Ouch. There, I said it!

Sadly, you see, the Westernized Jesus most of us serve today in the church growth movement has evolved into a promoter of North American business values where bigger is better, more is better than less, and success is achieved when we build buildings that are impressive in size, when cash is flowing like milk and honey, and when weekend attendance numbers are breaking new records!

As I see it, to make the mission of the church of North America conform to the kingdom principles Wimber talks about here, pastors and ministry overseers must, first and foremost, address this hideous side of self-promotion that lies deep within the bowels of the church growth movement. In truth, the 3-B pastor who secretly hungers for self-recognition must be stopped cold in his or her tracks. The 3-Bs that are driving so many church leaders through the pursuit of self-edifying glory has to be destroyed!

Interestingly enough, Wimber was known in his day as a church growth proponent. Yet, as we see in his quote above, church growth principles never trumped his passion for the fine art of living and ministering in the kingdom life of Christ. In truth, when he gave his life to Christ back in 1963, he quickly learned that the way of life to which he was accustomed needed to die so that he could learn to walk in the kingdom ways of God.

For me, a recovering 3-B pastor who no longer wants to measure success (or failure) in my church by looking at (B)uildings, (B)ucks, and(B)utts in the seats, I find it refreshing to hear John's words once more:

> Our primary aim in life is to love and glorify God and expand his kingdom in relevant ways in the time allotted us. As communities of the King, Vineyard churches should model what the kingdom looks like when God has his way with a group of people.

Thanks, John. This recovering 3-B pastor really needs to remember that!

PRAYER

God, my confession as a recovering 3-B pastor is humbling indeed. I'm certain that John Wimber never expected the church family that he began to become more consumed in growing and expanding the church than we are in simply being kingdom people doing our very best to follow Jesus wherever he might go. Spirit, allow us the grace to throw away the 3-Bs and begin measuring our success in ministry once again by using standards found in the Scriptures instead of twenty-first century books on successful church growth. For your name's sake. Amen!

QUESTIONS FOR YOU TO PONDER

- What changes need to occur in our approach to pastoral ministry and mission today?
- Am I measuring my success or failure using kingdom principles found in the New Testament or am I using Americanized business models where growth and expansion is the *end all* toward success?

So, what is God speaking to you today as you ponder the *Wisdom of Wimber?*

Mission 101: Finding Out What the Father Is Doing

To continue Jesus ministry requires that we adopt his methods. Unfortunately, Christians in the West would rather implement programs. We are blind to our mechanistic assumptions when we reduce ministry to reproducible components and try to apply them indiscriminately. There is nothing wrong, for instance, with a tool for witnessing like *The Four Spiritual Laws*. It helps believers communicate biblical truth, but should we use it every time? No. We must ask what is appropriate in each situation and learn the art of listening, even as Jesus modeled (Jn. 5:19; 30).

An early slogan we liked was, "What is the Father doing?" We tried to enter each ministry situation with that question foremost in our minds. Our experiences in spiritual gifts were an attempt to discern what the Father was up to. Whether the situation was evangelism, healing, budgeting for the poor, or sending a couple across country to plant a church, the important thing was to ask the Father what he was doing.[61]

Let's be honest.

Most human beings prefer it when everything we do in life is relatively safe and predictable. Oh sure, all of us like a bit of excitement in our lives, but even those daredevils amongst us who enjoy living on the cutting edge of life still do their very best to reduce risk, keeping things under their control, whenever and wherever possible. So it is with us church leaders and our approach to doing ministry and mission in the name of Jesus.

Now, please. Don't get me wrong. As I see it, there's nothing overtly wrong when those of us in church leadership lay out our prayerfully constructed ministry or mission plans and then systematically work those plans. God did give us our brains and our ability to reason.

But here's the rub.

As Wimber points out in the quote above, it's so easy for us to go astray in Christian mission when we church leaders choose to take things into our own hands, re-making the New Testament goal of following Jesus into a systematic program to be followed rather than a living-and-breathing relationship that needs nurturing.

In truth, what Jesus models for us in the gospels is a life-style in ministry that, quite honestly, is frightening to most of us who relish keeping our lives orderly and under our own control. Following Jesus, you see, as demonstrated by those living in the first century, didn't mean grabbing life by the horns and getting things done, come hell or high water. Nor did it mean that you and I, as leaders, are called to get creative, using our vain imagination to develop mission plans, which have at their core, our insatiable drive to control things as we want them to go!

If you've been a reader of my blog (www.pastorboller.com) in recent years, you'll know that God has spoken very clearly to me, reminding me of all the many years I spent so much time, energy, and resources, assembling nice and neat programming for my church. Programming that looked good on paper, but quite honestly, was birthed out of my own self-consumed interests and desires to do some impressive things in ministry so that my church would grow in numbers.

There, I said it.

I am thankful for the reminder that Jesus isn't looking for men and women who will bring their own agendas into his ministry. As I see it, Jesus is not looking for dynamic leaders, but for humble folks who know full well their weaknesses and susceptibility toward controlling things. As Wimber so succinctly states here, Jesus is recruiting men and women who will honestly spend their days in ministry learning the fine art of finding out what the Father is doing and, then, in humility and obedience, going and doing it! And then, if there's any time left over after doing that, we spend the remainder of that time encouraging others to do the same.

PRAYER

Father, I humbly confess that it's so easy to begin ministry by saying that I'm looking for what you are doing, but, then, I go off on my own, allowing personal agendas to rule the way I act on that mission. In the process, Lord, I end up doing things in ministry that simply seem good to me instead of waiting and watching for your will to be done. Spirit, come direct me into the ways of Jesus, where he always preferred and deferred to the expressed will of the Father. For your name's sake. Amen!

QUESTIONS FOR YOU TO PONDER

- Where am I following systematic programming ministry efforts rather than waiting upon the Father, asking him, as Jesus did, to show us his will and kingdom-directed interests?
- Am I taking the necessary time needed to develop the relational aspects of "following Jesus" or am I moving forward in mission and ministry, using my own self-directed, self-centered initiatives?

So, what is God speaking to you today as you ponder the *Wisdom of Wimber?*

BLESSED ARE THE FLEXIBLE

But whatever you do, don't hold onto things for their own sake. Programs are means to an end. Evaluate their effectiveness. Keep what works; get rid of what doesn't. Do whatever is necessary to help the church of Jesus Christ to advance.[62]

As I see it, Wimber, at his very core, was a churchman. He was a pastor, a shepherd who loved Jesus and the church that is called by his name.

Yes, Wimber was a well-known author, a highly sought-after conference speaker, and a visionary leader who birthed a movement of churches. But deep down, John and Carol Wimber were lovers of the church, and wanted to do everything and anything they could to help the church at large be all Jesus hopes it could be.

So because of that deep love for Jesus and his church, there was nothing sacred in church for Wimber except Jesus. As you can see from the quote above, for Wimber, flexibility was the key to pastoral ministry. Thus, when it came to helping pastors act on the mission Jesus gives his church, John insisted that the only important thing in church life that really matters is making sure that we are keeping the main thing, the main thing.

And for Wimber, the main thing for him as a functioning pastor was being radically obedient to Jesus, making sure that he was always flexible, keeping in step with the Master, rather than falling into the temptation of doing things just to do them. Over time, this flexibility and his radical obedience to Jesus cost Wimber a lot. In a world where it's so easy for pastors to read the latest "how-to" book on church growth and then go establish a bunch of programming so that our churches will be able to keep up with the latest fads in American church life, Wimber would buck that system and ask us if we were doing what the Father had asked

183

us to do. When others would tell him that it wasn't practical to focus so much attention on the Holy Spirit, warning him that it wouldn't be comfortable for many evangelical pastors, once again, he would throw out pre-conditioned programming standards to do what he sensed the Father was doing.

At times, he was criticized sharply for taking so many risks with the ministries God had placed into his hands. At a time in life when other well-established pastors would rest on their laurels, keeping the status-quo whenever and wherever possible, Wimber always seemed to be looking and listening to God, doing his very best to make sure he and his church were always keeping in step with the Spirit and not just "doing church" for "church-sake."

One of Wimber's favorite quips was: "Faith is spelled R-I-S-K." So for him, it was a sin to keep pouring time, energy, and resources into a well-worn program in his church, particularly if he was confident that the program was stealing life from people rather producing life in the church. Thus, programming in church ministry was always being evaluated when you were around him. Flexibility was the key. If something was working; it stayed. But if it wasn't, he had no problem cutting it, even if that ministry or program had been in the church for decades.

I guess, in truth, Wimber was a reformer, a pastor who loved the church dearly but was never impressed by its cultural presentation. A man of passion who would rather be found guilty of following Jesus than standing around doing things just because that's the way we've always done it.

Hmm. Maybe we need a few more Jesus-loving, church-loving reformers like Wimber in today's church? Anybody wanna sign up? Remember, blessed are the flexible for they won't be bent out of shape!

PRAYER

Father, over time, it's very easy to remove risk from our work and just go with the program. Thank you that in John Wimber, I never saw a man who was satisfied with just "doing church," but one who demanded of himself that he was always listening and looking for what the Father was doing. Spirit, empower me to be a risk-taker for Jesus, even when others say that I might be rocking the boat too much. For your name's sake. Amen!

QUESTIONS FOR YOU TO PONDER

- Where have I allowed the status quo to lull me to sleep?
- Have I lost my ability to be flexible? Am I too interested in playing it safe when compared to my drive to always be doing what the Father is doing?
- What might it look like right now for me to step out in faith on those things that I sense God asking me to do?

So, what is God speaking to you today as you ponder the *Wisdom of Wimber*?

Like young Timothy, we all need to be encouraged to persevere in the ministry to which God has called us. We can become discouraged and fearful when we face the inevitable hardships, resistant or hostile people, and frustrations of the ministry. These are simply the realities of ministry. Yet God the Holy Spirit, the same Spirit who calls us to serve God, can renew our strength and remind us of the true and eternal value of our work.

This is an exciting time in history to serve God. Our enemy, Satan, has overplayed his hand by brutalizing the people of the earth for centuries. The earth and its people are crying out for relief and salvation from the evil forces and destruction which continue to victimize them. God wants to use us to continue Jesus' ministry of Liberation! To the sick and diseased, Jesus brought healing; to the spiritually oppressed, Jesus brought deliverance; to those separated from God, he brought forgiveness and restoration. It was always Jesus' plan to continue to vanquish the power of the evil one by using flesh and blood people like you and me. There is no greater calling![63]

So, what do you want to do with the rest of your life?

I remember attending my very first Vineyard healing conference in Mansfield, Ohio, in March of 1985. Our church in Evanston, IL, had first come into contact with John Wimber and the Vineyard churches just the year before (1984). It turned out that one of our senior pastors at the time was suffering from a serious heart disease and a relative of his who lived in southern California recommended that we check out this guy named John Wimber who had a healing ministry in Anaheim, California.

Our church at this time was made up of about one hundred or so fairly typical Bible-believing, Jesus-loving twenty-somethings, gathering to worship in the northern suburbs of Chicago. To be honest, we all believed in healing that came from Jesus, but we were just a bit skeptical of those wild-eyed Pentecostals with their name-it-claim-it healing ministries like the ones we had seen on TV. But this John Wimber fellow surprised us! He just didn't seem to fit the typical stereotypes we knew that we wanted to avoid. So after several months of checking Wimber and the Vineyard out, we invited a couple of his associates to come to Evanston in the fall of 1984 to introduce us to some of the kingdom basics that Wimber had been teaching successfully for several years at Fuller Seminary in California. Many of those basics we began learning back then are the same subjects we're discussing here in this book! Our church family so enjoyed this first exposure to Wimber's material, we decided to send a couple of our pastors out west to attend his first "Signs & Wonders & Church Growth" conference held in January 1985.

Suffice to say that our pastors came back hooked for life. Wimber's sound biblical approach to the supernatural wonders of God was nothing less than impressive and our church in Evanston, IL, bought in lock, stock, and barrel. By March of that year, several of us were invited to attend a leadership conference to be held in Mansfield, Ohio. The main speaker was one of John's associates. So Sandy and I headed east to Ohio, not really certain what we'd find as we attended this weekend conference.

As I sat there listening to Blaine Cook, one of Wimber's associates, teach about the kingdom of God, my heart started to stir. Sandy and I had been Christians most of our lives, but had never really been exposed to the concept that regular, everyday Christians, living in our day, were called and commissioned to step into Jesus' kingdom ministry, where healing the sick, casting out darkness, and speaking words of hope became our job description as followers of Christ. Like Wimber's quote above says:

> This is an exciting time in history to serve God. Our enemy, Satan, has overplayed his hand by brutalizing the people of

187

the earth for centuries. The earth and its people are crying out for relief and salvation from the evil forces and destruction which continue to victimize them. God wants to use us to continue Jesus ministry of Liberation! To the sick and diseased, Jesus brought healing; to the spiritually oppressed, Jesus brought deliverance; to those separated from God, he brought forgiveness and restoration. It was always Jesus' plan to continue to vanquish the power of the evil one by using flesh and blood people like you and me. There is no greater calling!

By the conference's end, Sandy and I were both convinced that we needed to spend the remainder of our days here on earth joining with Jesus in his mission to bring hope and promise to this darkened world around us. Cook ended the conference by calling people forward who sensed that they were to spend the rest of their days serving Jesus in this capacity. I remember going forward and standing in the ministry line that Sunday morning. I had closed my eyes and had placed my hands in front of me, palms up. My prayer was "Oh Lord, here I am. I'm just a fat guy from Evanston, IL, managing a Logos Christian Bookstore. I don't have much to offer you, Lord. I'm not seminary trained. I'm not all that biblically literate, I'm just a guy from Iowa, now living in Illinois, with a music education degree that I'm not even using, but here I am. Use me."

With my eyes closed, I felt the hand of someone covering my heart. I heard the voice of Cook say, "Lord, put a hook in his heart!" I felt a rush of power in my chest. I thought I might fall down, but I kept my cool (like the staunch Presbyterian I'd learned to become over the years) and just let God do whatever he wanted to do. No other words were spoken, but deep inside, I knew that the Holy Spirit was ordaining me into Jesus' kingdom ministry. Suddenly, I started to weep uncontrollably. Wow, was I embarrassed! Yet I knew it was God stirring something inside me that, even to this day, I know is still there and is still very pro-active.

For about four months after that power encounter with Jesus,

I had a hard time not crying whenever I heard the name Jesus spoken. Embarrassing as that was, I knew that I was in a season where God was inviting me into things I'd always believed were there, but until I heard it talked about from a biblical perspective from guys like Wimber and his friends, I never believed folks like me could actually play.

Hmm. Even as I write this, I wonder how many of you out there today reading my words, need to hear a similar invitation into the kingdom ministry and mission of Jesus of Nazareth? An invitation, just like the one I heard from the Holy Spirit back in March of 1985 in Mansfield, Ohio.

"Lord, put a hook in the heart!"

Ohh-ohh. You need a hanky? I certainly hope so!

PRAYER

Father God, there's still a lot of kingdom work out there waiting for those who will respond to your invitation. I, for one, Lord, am thankful for your invitation you extended to me in March of 1985 and I bless your holy name for the empowerment of your Spirit, which has allowed me to stay on course for nearly thirty years now. Keep leading, Jesus, and I will follow. For your name's sake. Amen!

QUESTIONS FOR YOU TO PONDER

- So what will it look and feel like for me today to know with certainty that Jesus still has his kingdom hook in my heart and that he has no plans to ever let go?
- Where is he leading me today, and am I willing to fully trust him as he leads?

So, what is God speaking to you today as you ponder the *Wisdom of Wimber?*

AND THEN THE END WILL COME

Like many Christians in the last ten to twenty years, I spent a lot of time and energy learning about Jesus' second coming, the rapture, and tribulation. I was weaned as a baby Christian on all the best known teachers of the second coming of Jesus. It was and still is a subject that truly excites me! However, after several years of hearing many debates on whether there would be a rapture before, during or after the tribulation, I simply "wore out" waiting for Jesus. I decided it was time I seriously looked into the bulk of Scriptures dealing with the Christian's lifestyle and ministry.

I discovered that Jesus said this regarding the end times: "And this gospel of the kingdom will be preached in the *whole world* as a testimony to all nations, and *then the end will come.*" (Matt. 24:14) Jesus clearly links the end times to the completion of a task. That task is the extending of God's rule upon the earth in the words and works of the kingdom! This message and ministry of the gospel is to be taken to the whole world by each generation of the church until he comes! Jesus does want us to be committed to his Second Coming and be prepared at all times. But he also wants us to be committed to speaking his words and doing his works until he appears![64]

Over the years, I must admit that I've experienced much of what Wimber talks about here. Ever since the release of Hal Lindsey's classic book, *The Late Great Planet Earth* in 1970, Christians have been abuzz about the end of the world as we know it and how that plays into the second coming of Christ. Back then, I remember some of my more conservative friends being very frustrated with me because I wouldn't read the book, *88 Reasons Why the Rapture Will Be in 1988*. After managing a Christian bookstore for so many years prior to that and seeing a long litany of second coming books bite the dust, my sarcastic side seemed to show when I told my friends that I was going to wait and buy the book in 1989, because then, I would be able to purchase it for pennies on the dollar!

More recently, the *Left Behind* novel series has served to stir the flames of second coming imaginations for so many believers. And does anybody remember Y2K? Or what about the recent 2012 Mayan calendar debate? Gosh, even the godless sinners who run some of the major Hollywood movie studios got caught up with that one, didn't they?

So, as I see it, Wimber was right. When it comes to our limited time here on planet earth, I often ponder if Satan has his dirty little hands in all of this? Think about it with me for a minute, will you? Let's say, for example, if the devil really wanted to accomplish something of worth for the kingdom of darkness, what better way could there be than to get a great majority of the good guys and gals so focused on the end that they neglect to *do* the very thing that Jesus says will actually usher in the end?

Hmm. Almost makes you wanna laugh doesn't it?

But, friends, this is serious business. Way too serious for us to chuckle over how distracted Satan can get us if we don't pay attention to what is real and what is just a mirage. The second coming is set in stone. A done deal. In heaven, there is no uncertainty or doubt about it. No worry there that the end will turn out differently than God the Father has already planned it to be.

I love the line Jack Hayford reportedly uses when asked to lay out all the gory details surrounding the coming of the end. "Pre-trib? Post-trib? Mid-trib," Jack quips, "All I know is that the Bible says when Jesus comes, we go!"

Somehow, I think Wimber and Hayford, good friends for a good many years, hold the key to how we Christians should approach this second-coming dilemma in which we often find ourselves. As I see it, let's not worry about all the sordid details, but let's just get about the business of loving the hell out of folks around us. So much love and so much care that it will be almost impossible for people in our communities to go to hell. So much of Jesus, so much of his kingdom mercy, deliverance, and healing, it will be next to impossible for the devil to slip in there and pull anyone off track.

Wha-da-ya-say, church? Let's get busy just doin' the commission and spend much less time figuring out the fine print! For Jesus' sake!

PRAYER

Jesus, I believe you said it rightly. No one, including you or the angels in heaven, know the day or the hour of your return (Matthew 24: 36). But, Father, for those of us who live on this planet today, help us to keep our eyes and ears ready for that return, while keeping our focus on doing the very work of the kingdom that Jesus says will usher in that same end we all are looking forward to. For your name's sake. Amen!

QUESTIONS FOR YOU TO PONDER

- What needs to change in my approach to the "second coming" of Jesus?
- Am I caught up in the theology or the countless opinions surrounding this important future event, or am I devoting myself fully to the work of the kingdom?
- Am I keeping my eyes and ears focused on Jesus and the work yet to be done before he returns?

So, what is God speaking to you today as you ponder the *Wisdom of Wimber?*

ON UNITY

To be committed to God is

to be committed to His community, the Church.

Loving Others: Agreement or Unity

I think we underestimate the power and importance of loving each other. Consistent love for other Christians is key to a healthy spiritual life because loving fellowship is God's prescribed environment for growth. This kind of love is based on commitment to God Himself. To be committed to God is to be committed to His community, the Church. This is not a commitment to the theory of the church, but to an actual body of other fallible, imperfect people.[65]

One of the key driving components inside Wimber and the work he did for God's kingdom was his amazing ability to love and appreciate the larger body of Christ. Over the years, I believe many have forgotten how careful he was to never speak negatively toward other Christians, even when some of those same brothers and sisters were spouting off publicly with all kinds of negative comments concerning John and the work he was doing for Jesus.

As John states in the quote above, "Consistent love for other Christians is key to a healthy spiritual life" can be difficult. Loving the whole body of Christ is not an easy thing. Loving another brother or sister in your own denomination or in your own church community can be very difficult indeed!

Sadly, in many churches today, the hope of walking in consistent love, never having a major conflict in the midst of church life, is either uninformed at best, or foolish at worst. Gather two people together for the purposes of worshipping God and serving Jesus and before you can say, "Hallelujah," you'll have at least two different opinions on how best to do just that! Add in another few hundred sincere worshippers and you can have major conflict brewing in a matter of hours!

As we begin this section of our book on the subject of unity within the body of Christ, let's get very practical here. It's not easy living in peace with our Christian brothers and sisters. But yet, as the Bible points out, Jesus does command us, as his followers, to love one another just as he loves us (see John 13: 34-35).

Jesus has commanded us to love others as we love ourselves and we all know how very difficult that is. Wimber's daughter-in-law, Christy Wimber, shared with us on one of her trips to Cedar Rapids, that there is a difference between trying to find agreement with one another as Christians, and God's ability to grant us his unity. Finding total agreement with others in the body of Christ is nearly impossible. Over the years, she has come to the conclusion that it's not even desirable to look for agreement at times, because agreement means that everyone must agree to build community. Unity, on the other hand, means that we are choosing oneness of heart, mind, and spirit, despite our varying opinions or lack of total agreement on all issues.

I like that. And as I see it, so does Jesus.

Lasting peace, you see, within the larger body of Christ, is a tough thing to find when all we will accept is agreement on difficult subjects. But just imagine how beautiful the church might look if you and I would begin asking the Lord to help us find unity in our relationships instead of agreement. When unity becomes our goal, you and I can strongly disagree on certain subjects, but at the end of the day, if we both claim Jesus as our leader, I think he can bring unity that truly binds us together as one.

I recall, with great warmness in my heart, my years of working with the men's ministry, Promise Keepers (PK). I remember attending one of our PK conferences in Minneapolis. Our team was invited to speak at an African-American church, and as a white man, I felt just a bit uncomfortable in surroundings that were different than my own. I think one of the men from the church recognized my un-comfortableness and he walked right up to me and said, "Welcome, my good friend. I want you to feel right at home here in our church. You see, if God is your Father, Jesus is your Savior, and the Holy Spirit is your friend, then I *must* be your long-lost brother!" To that, I believe Jesus would say…"Amen and amen."

PRAYER

Father, it's difficult, if not impossible, to look for "agreement" amongst men and women with so many differing views on life and ministry. But, thank you, while I may not always find agreement amongst my brothers and sisters, your hand can help us find unity, where our common denominator becomes God as our Father, Christ as our Savior, and the Holy Spirit as our Guide. For your name's sake. Amen!

QUESTIONS FOR YOU TO PONDER

- What needs to change in my approach to loving the whole church?
- Am I fully aware of, and acting upon, the call to unity that Jesus demands from his followers?
- Is my day-to-day Christian life contributing toward the unity of the church or is it serving to divide and isolate brothers and sisters in Christ?

So, what is God speaking to you today as you ponder the *Wisdom of Wimber*?

UNITY: A MATURE COMMITMENT OF LOVE

Many of us treat church life like immature adolescents. From other Christians we want thrills, constant exhilaration and to have our needs met. When Christian brothers and sisters fall short of our expectations, when they are boring and imperfect and fail to meet our needs for strokes, we pout, turn away and isolate ourselves from them. Jesus calls us to mature commitment of love for His people—the very people in our fellowship![66]

Paul, in his first letter to the Corinthian church (13: 11) said, "When I was a child, I talked like a child, I thought like a child, I reasoned like a child. When I became a man, I put the ways of childhood behind me."

Sadly, as Wimber points out here, too many Christians across the fruited plain of America, treat our commitment to the body of Christ much like we treat our television sets. There we sit on Sunday mornings, watching the show on the stage. If we don't like what we see or we determine that the programming for the day is not feeding us, we tune out. Over time, many Christians eventually switch channels (churches); and if that doesn't work, we stop watching TV (attending church) all together!

Hmm.

Now don't get me wrong. As a recovering 3-B pastor, one who no longer wants to define success in my church by measuring (B)uilding size, counting (B)ucks in the offering plate, and by increasing the number of (B)utts in the seats, I'm aware that Americanized church plays right into a keeping-the-consumer-happy mindset. Now that I've punched in thirty years of pastoral ministry on my time card, I can sadly look back now and regret all the ways I focused on keeping the crowd satisfied over the years while trying my best to build the big, successful Vineyard church of which I always dreamed.

But as I look back at Wimber, the founding pastor of the Vineyard, I realize that he never really commissioned us to build big Vineyard churches, but positioned us to listen carefully for what the Father was doing, and then step out in faithfulness, completing the task or tasks Jesus assigns to our lives.

As I write this book, the *Wisdom of Wimber*, I'm struck once again on how much John and Carol Wimber loved the church that they pastored. For him, the Anaheim Vineyard was not a monument to his church-planting prowess, but a group of people gathered together sovereignly by the Lord, to model what a community of believers might look like who are doing their very best to follow obediently wherever the Master might lead.

Pastors, might I recommend that you and I lay down a lot of our driving, striving efforts to build successful ministries for our name's sake, and simply learn the lesson John and Carol modeled so well? Living out, as pastoral shepherds, a *"mature commitment of love for his people–the very people in our fellowship!"*

Who knows, maybe if a few of us pastors will stop the 3-B programming and get back to the ancient pastoral work of simply caring for parishioners, they will begin to put down their TV remotes and join us, hand in hand, in building the God-worshipping, Christ-following, Spirit-directed community of faith we all hope to see.

PRAYER

Father, I confess my childish behavior that keeps me always focused on what's best for me. Spirit, help me, as Wimber used to say, to grow up before I grow old. Empower me to faithfulness and long obedience in the same direction. For your name's sake. Amen!

QUESTIONS FOR YOU TO PONDER

- Finding true unity in the body of Christ takes a Christ-empowered long-suffering where I let go of my "me-first" attitude and begin to become otherly, caring for others as much as I care for myself. Am I willing to go there?

- Am I willing to not quickly "change channels" when I get frustrated or bored? Will I be willing to enter into the sometimes-difficult process of building true community amongst brothers and sisters in Christ, for the sake of his glorious kingdom?

So what is God speaking to you today as you ponder the *Wisdom of Wimber?*

THE MINISTRY OF CARE AND LOVING OTHERS

The truth is that the Lord's work is humble caring.

Paul (says), "Do nothing from selfishness for conceit, but in humility count others better than yourselves."

The "humility" that Paul refers to here is not a groveling concession that everyone else is more gifted, more beautiful, and more worthwhile than you are. It refers to status. The servants in God's household treat everyone else as if they had a higher status in the kingdom. A servant takes care of others first, then himself. The essence of servanthood is to live out your life for someone else. That's the kind of life Jesus led, and that's the kind of life we are called to as believers.

This is what authentic ministry is – caring and loving others.[67]

u·ni·ty

a *noun.* the state of being united or joined as a whole.

Unity is a word we like to use a lot in church life, but sadly, it is not something that occurs often.

It's very common in the DNA of each of us to find our unique place in the world, establishing ourselves as independent, self-sufficient men or women. In the process, humankind has this uncanny way of separating ourselves from others, keeping our day-to-day existence at a distance from the rest of the human race. And while psychologists will tell us that it's important for each of us to have our unique identity, that same drive to become people unto ourselves can also serve to push us away from the shared benefits found from living in close contact with others.

I find it interesting that in the Bible, we see God speaking this truth to us in the very first chapters of the Bible, telling us that it's not good for a man (or woman) to be alone. Yet, over the centuries, since Jesus of Nazareth set up his church, we've now become one of the most divided (and divisive?) organizations known to man!

According to the World Christian Encyclopedia (year 2001 version), global Christianity has 33,820 denominations.[68] A more recent report[69] from another reliable source suggests that there are now at least 41,000 different sects of Christianity across the planet. Yikes.

This information reminds me of the old joke:

> There was a man who was stranded on a desert island for many, many years. One day, while strolling along the beach, he spotted a ship in the distance. This had never happened in all the time he was on the island, so he was very excited about the chance of being rescued. Immediately, he built a fire on the beach and generated as much smoke as possible. It worked! Soon, the ship was heading his way. When the ship was close enough to the island, a dinghy was dispatched to investigate the situation. The man on the island was overjoyed with the chance to be rescued and met his saviors as they landed.
>
> After some preliminary conversation the man in charge asked the man on the island how he had survived for so many years. The man replied by telling of his exploits for food and how he was able to make a fine house to live in. In fact, the man said, "You can see my home from here. It's up there on the ridge." He pointed the men in the direction of his home. They looked up and saw three buildings. They inquired about the building next to the man's house and he replied, "That's my church - I go there to worship on Sundays."
>
> When asked about the third building, the man replied, "That's where I used to go to church!"

Ba-boom!

So what can be done to counter this splintered approach to our shared Christian faith? As I see it, it goes back to what Wimber talks about in the quote above, "The truth is that the Lord's work is humble caring."

Christ-centered Christianity just can't be lived out by ourselves. A true Christian is a caring person, always looking to serve the needs of others around us. As a result, true Christianity is meant to be lived out in "community." For heaven's sake, even the word itself (community) speaks of common-unity.

Guess it's time for a generation of Jesus followers to stop the madness. Rather than shooting for a new high in different denominations (anybody want to go for 42,000?), how about if we go back to working on humble caring and simple servanthood toward one another. Anybody wanna play?

PRAYER

Lord Jesus, I'm saddened at the way we've behaved over the last 2,000 years. We've taken your call for oneness in Christ and divided ourselves now into 41,000 different sects. And then we wonder why the rest of the world isn't running to our doorsteps looking for the "unity" we claim we have. It's time to change, Lord. Holy Spirit, come. Heal our wounds and bring us "common-unity." For your name's sake. Amen!

QUESTIONS FOR YOU TO PONDER

- What am I doing to repair the breach in the church of Jesus Christ?
- Am I looking for creative ways to unify the church through acts of compassion and humble service or am I just another instrument that serves to further divide the body of Christ from within?

So, what is God speaking to you today as you ponder the *Wisdom of Wimber*?

Years ago I consulted with a young man (not in the Vineyard) during a conference in the Midwest. He had been an evangelist in a certain denomination for several years, and had wearied of that, and wanted to pastor. His denominational leader had said to him, "Why don't you go up to this community here. We have a little church that hasn't done too well. Go up there and see what you can get stirred up, and if you do well, then I'll give you a more choice position later on in a bigger church."

We met at a restaurant and he brashly told me what he was going to do. He wanted my advice on how to "jump start" the church.

I said, "I can't do that."

"Why?"

"Because there's no integrity in what you're doing. You're going up to that little community like a gigolo, pretending you love this part of the bride of Christ. You're going to have intercourse with her in hopes of having children, but you have no intention of raising them. No intention of loving, protecting, or caring for her. You just want to have a few babies with her so you can get a chance to have some other babies somewhere else. I can't bless that, and I don't want any part of what you're about to do."[70]

The church in America is in the midst of a severe identity crisis. This crisis has been going on now for some time. Wimber's story from the early 1980s points to the crisis being in full bloom even back then.

The crisis, you ask?

As I see it, we simply have forgotten who Jesus commissioned his shepherds to be.

Sadly, over the last fifty years, our American business culture has trumped nearly everything we do in church life; and we baby boomers, the generation to which I belong, decided, long ago, to buy into three underlying truths that drive our American economy.

1. Truth #1: Bigger is always better.
2. Truth #2: Success can always be measured in numbers.
3. Truth #3: Winning isn't everything...it's the *only* thing.

Take these three business truths that drive American capitalism, surround them with a few Scriptures hand-picked from the New Testament, and there you have it. The foundational planks to a church culture that produces a "gigolo" pastor like the man who was confronted by Wimber back in the 1980s. Today, I prefer to use the term I've referred to earlier, the 3-B pastor, one who has given himself/herself over to measuring his/her success in ministry by using three major components; (B)uilding size, (B)ucks in the offering, and the number of (B)utts in the seats.

As I see it, Jesus of Nazareth, points to the "gigolo" pastor or the 3-B pastor by calling them a "hired hand." In John's gospel, (10: 11-13) Jesus talks quite plainly about it.

> I am the good shepherd. The good shepherd lays down his life for the sheep. The hired hand is not the shepherd and does not own the sheep. So when he sees the wolf coming, he abandons the sheep and runs away. Then the wolf attacks the flock and scatters it. The man runs away because he is a hired hand and cares nothing for the sheep.

Ouch.

One very well-known church leader in America recently said that he believes Christians should strike the word "shepherd" from our ministry vocabulary. "That word needs to go away," the leader is quoted as saying, "It was culturally relevant in the time of Jesus, but it's not culturally relevant anymore."

Yikes. Are you serious?

Remove the word "shepherd" from our ministry vocabulary? I guess we should then proceed with this leader's suggestion and rewrite Psalm 23 so it reads, "The Lord is my CEO, I will never want for business leads?"

My fellow men and women of the cloth, this nonsense has got to go! How about if we throw off the heavy weights of being a 3-B pastor, a CEO, or an executive-manager for the church, and we take back the original shepherding call that Jesus modeled to his generation?

Hmm. Shepherd or hired hand? Which title is on *your* resume?

PRAYER

Father, as a baby-boomer-pastor who got caught up very early in ministry with the 3-Bs, I now forsake my ungodly ways. I refuse to measure my success in ministry, or my church's success in ministry, by using components that you never used in your generation. As a pastor, called by your name, restore my identity as a pastoral shepherd who faithfully serves under the good shepherd, caring for souls along the way, one person at a time. Nothing more. Nothing less. For your name's sake. Amen!

QUESTIONS FOR YOU TO PONDER

- If loving the sheep and laying down my life for the sheep was the gold standard Jesus set for pastoral ministry, how can I jettison other ministry models that my society forces upon the church?
- What might the church of Jesus Christ look like in America if more pastors stepped away from the 3-Bs and became exclusively obedient to Jesus' commission of shepherding the sheep?

So, what is God speaking to you today as you ponder the *Wisdom of Wimber*?

Jesus said, "I will build my church, and the gates of Hades will not overcome it" (Mt. 16:18). Peter preached, "God says, I will pour out my Spirit on all people" (Acts 2:17). Evidence confirms that Jesus and Peter's prophecies are being fulfilled. Despite the darkness (2 Tim. 2:19), Jesus is building his church, the Spirit is being poured out all over the world. The percentage of earth's population that is Christian is growing.

Paul said the church reveals something of the nature of God (Eph. 3:10). God reconciles the many from different cultures into the one body. Jesus will build his church "from every people group" to use my late friend Donald McGavran's favorite phrase (Rev. 7:9).[71]

He has sounded forth the trumpet that shall never call retreat;
He is sifting out the hearts of men before his judgment-seat:
Oh, be swift, my soul, to answer him! Be jubilant, my feet!
Our God is marching on.
Glory! Glory! Hallelujah! Glory! Glory! Hallelujah!
Glory! Glory! Hallelujah! Our God is marching on.[72]

In truth, from the days of John the Baptist to today, the kingdom of God has never lost traction. The trumpet of Christ's redemptive power was sounded from the empty tomb 2,000 years ago, and now, the entire world is being given ample opportunity to answer that same redemptive call.

Calvinist theology tells me that Christ's commission will be completed whether I participate or not. Arminian theology teaches me that God himself has chosen to defer his power, in part, to human will, and that I must play my important role in God's plan for his truth and salvation to be spread across the nations.

Call me crazy, but I believe strongly both ways. Yes and amen. God works his sovereign plan in his grace alone; and I have the unique honor of seeing my work for him play a major role in his salvation plan for planet earth.

Thus, on some days, when I feel as though my work for Christ is never sufficient enough, I need to be reminded that I can rest assured in the sovereignty of God. He will always be able to trump anything or everything (good, bad, or ugly). I will ever have to offer the King of kings. On other days, however, as I lay in bed, resting in that same assuredness that God's sovereignty will take care of my neighbor's slothfulness, I need to get my butt out of bed and remember that my salvation has a bigger purpose in this world beyond simply saving me from my sin. Yes, Marty, God wants me to get up out of my slumber and go love "the hell" out of my neighbor, for heaven's sake!

As I see it, Wimber was great at reminding us of how big God is and how powerful his sovereign hand can be in our midst. At the same time, John was always chiding us that everyone needs to play, reminding us that while God never needs me to save the world, he truly loves it when I get about the business of working alongside him as he does that very thing.

Which brings us to Jesus' call for unity in his church, particularly as that unity Jesus calls for plays such an important role in the conversion of the lost. Look at what Jesus prays here in John 17, verses 20-23 in the Message:

I'm praying not only for them
But also for those who will believe in me
Because of them and their witness about me.
The goal is for all of them to become one heart and mind—
Just as you, Father, are in me and I in you,
So they might be one heart and mind with us.
Then the world might believe that you, in fact, sent me.
The same glory you gave me, I gave them,
So they'll be as unified and together as we are—
I in them and you in me.
Then they'll be mature in this oneness,

And give the godless world evidence
That you've sent me and loved them
In the same way you've loved me.

Now, keep in mind that Calvinist theology would say that God needs no help from his followers when it comes to convincing folks that Jesus is God's Son and the Savior of the world. But here's the rub. Jesus seems to be saying here that the world (i.e., the lost) will have a better chance believing in Jesus, if and when they see Jesus' followers living in the same one heart and mind that Jesus and the Father live in!

Yikes! Now that, my friends, can be one scary proposition. When the world sees us Jesus followers ranting and raving against one another, calling fellow brothers and sisters in Christ all types of names and spewing out all kinds of hatred toward others, folks in the world will see that and have a much harder time believing in Jesus than if they saw us living together in peace and tranquility.

Hmm.

Makes a pretty strong case, don't you think, for us Christians to clean up our act and stop all the monkey-business that surrounds our dislike and downright hatred for others who believe themselves to be Christians? Take a look at Facebook and see how nasty we Christians can be toward one another. Listen to a few sermons online or pick up one of the latest finger-pointing Christian books, which rants and raves about this pastor or that denomination that has gone off the deep end.

Folks, it's time to stop the madness and look carefully at what Jesus prays here. If indeed, our unity (or lack of it) plays that important of a role in worldwide evangelism, somebody needs to stand up and say, "Let's stop it kids, the world's watching...and they don't like what they're seeing right now!"

For heaven's sake, my friends, can't we Christians just all get along?

PRAYER

Father, I need to take seriously Jesus' prayer in John 17. If indeed, my dislike and disdain for another Christian brother or sister is seen by an unbeliever and then that activity of mine sours that non-believer's ability to trust in Jesus, shame on me! Spirit; change me from the inside-out, so that I make unity within the body of Christ vitally important to the kingdom cause of Christ around the world. For your name's sake. Amen!

QUESTIONS FOR YOU TO PONDER

- Am I aware of times when my sour attitude toward others in the body of Christ has actually served to turn off an unbeliever as they were considering Christ as Savior?
- If so, what can I do to correct that error?
- Am I doing everything I possibly can to speak well publicly of other Christians, even when I have major differences of opinion with them?

So, what is God speaking to you today as you ponder the *Wisdom of Wimber?*

LOVING THE THINGS THAT JESUS LOVES

Commitment to Christ is commitment to Christ's body.

When we make a commitment to Christ we make a commitment to his purpose in the world, which is to have a healthy, unified body, the people of God. A few years ago God showed me that I had sinned many times against the body of Christ. I had become judgmental of the larger body of Christ. I publicly repented of my judgmental and divisive attitude. God spoke to me about loving the things that he loves: *he loves his church.* He loves the whole church — Protestant and Catholic, Orthodox and Anabaptist.

Now by this I do not mean that he loves all the things different Christians believe and do. But in his heart Jesus deeply loves his body, those people who are born again of the Spirit of God and who know the Father.

We have been called to love the things that Jesus loves, so we have no choice but to love the whole church - even denominations whose beliefs we may not agree with or those parts we do not understand.[73]

It is one thing to say that I love the whole church of Jesus Christ, but quite another to actually find myself doing it.

Let's face it. There are so many areas of doctrine and practice where others are doing and saying things that rub us the wrong way. Gosh, I don't even have to step foot outside my own church to find folks who are believing things that I might believe to be near-heresy!

So what's a Bible-believing, God-worshipping, Jesus-following Christian to do?

As we discussed in an earlier chapter on unity, we noted that Christy Wimber suggests that we stop insisting on agreement in all of our relationships and focus more on unity instead. That's a great start! Kind of reminds me of the quote from St. Augustine, "In essentials, unity; in nonessentials, diversity; in all things, charity."

Here's another little secret I've found over the years, as I've worked with various parachurch ministries that were called to minister with pastors and leaders representing a wide variety of church denominations and theological beliefs.

First of all, when attempting to gather a broad network of pastors and leaders from a variety of backgrounds, it's always important to realize that there will be a cornucopia of doctrinal systems represented in our midst. As bridge-builders, working to build the oneness Jesus prays for in John 17: 20-23 (see our last chapter), I believe it's important to stay open and cordial to those in our midst who might hold to different doctrinal practices in their Christian faith than us.

I like the way my friend, Steve Sjogren, in his book *The Perfectly Imperfect Church*, addresses these doctrinal differences by separating them into three broad categories: 1) Essentials, 2) Traditions, and 3) Opinions.[74] Let me take the essence of what Steve says in his book on this subject and summarize it for you here.

"Essentials" are a very small circle of vital, life-giving kingdom-basics, rock-bottom biblical truths that we bridge-builders must never compromise on as we work hard to stretch our lives and faith toward others from a variety of backgrounds. "Traditions" compose a much larger circle of beliefs. Generally, they are the many practices we Christians have determined are important as we live out our faith in Christ. It's in this circle we find the rich diversity that makes up the denominational differences found in the larger church of Jesus Christ. Finally, "Opinions" are just that. And since they compose the largest circle of thought by far, "Opinions" will be abundant at every turn in church life. Unfortunately, the church becomes quite divided and often weakened, when we confuse Traditions with Essentials. Worse yet, Christians often take Opinions and allow them to divide us from other brothers and sisters in Christ, leaving us to go it alone in our faith journey in life.

FIVE ESSENTIALS OF CHRISTIANITY

To bring unity in the midst of our diversity, the ministries my wife and I now oversee (see www.pastorboller.com), offer these five "essentials" as the base from which we operate. We list them in the form of five basic questions, which if left unanswered, will leave all of us floating in a world of doctrinal confusion and uncertainty.[75]

1. Who is God?

We believe that there is one God and Creator, eternally existing in three persons: the Father, the Son, and the Holy Spirit (Deuteronomy 6:3-4).

2. What about the Bible?

We believe that the Bible is God's inspired and authoritative written revelation to us, containing his kingdom message of hope, love, and redemption to a lost and dying world (2 Timothy 3:16-17).

3. Who is Jesus of Nazareth?

We believe in the deity of our Lord Jesus Christ, his virgin birth, sinless life, miracles, death on the cross to provide for our redemption, bodily resurrection and ascension into heaven, present day ministry of intercession for us, and his second coming to earth in power and glory (Acts 4:10-12).

4. Who is the Holy Spirit?

We believe in the personality and deity of the Holy Spirit, that he performs the miracle of new birth, and indwells, equips and empowers us to walk with God, accomplishing the works of his kingdom through our humble service to him (John 14: 16-17).

5. What does all this mean for us?

We believe that we are created in the image of God, but because of our sin and selfishness, we become alienated from God. Only through abiding faith, trusting in Jesus Christ alone for our redemption, which is made possible by his atoning death on the cross and his resurrection, can true forgiveness of our sins be found and our lives be restored back with God (Ephesians 2:4-9).

So there you have it. The five essentials that can hopefully form the solid base on which many in the body of Christ can gather around. It's our belief that by laying out these five essentials, we can build a rock-solid foundation on which our Jesus-centered ministries will never stray. By holding to these kingdom-truths, while embracing the rich diversity of "traditions" and "opinions" in our midst, I believe that all of us can better discover the powerful "unity" Jesus prayed for in John 17.

PRAYER

Father, forgive me when I take my traditions, or worse yet, my opinions, and shape them into non-negotiable essentials, thus building walls that serve to unnecessarily separate me from my brothers and sisters in Christ. Give us unity in our essentials, so that we might better appreciate the diversity in our nonessentials. And most of all, Father, give us charity in all things. For your name's sake. Amen!

QUESTIONS FOR YOU TO PONDER

- Which pet opinions and rich traditions have I allowed to become non-negotiable essentials in my faith, thus making them something that I insist all other Christians must agree with before I will reach out in love?
- Am I truly willing, in the interest of fulfilling Jesus' prayer in John 17, to reduce my long list of essentials so that true Christ-centered unity might be found within the broader body of Christ?

So, what is God speaking to you today as you ponder the *Wisdom of Wimber*?

On Evangelism

...the Spirit empowers for a purpose – not just an experience.

POWER FOR A PURPOSE

In the Vineyard, we always placed a priority on being empowered by the Spirit to continue Jesus' ministry. But the Spirit empowers for a purpose – not just an experience. At times we almost lose the purpose; at times we seem to lose the power. From the beginning we have attempted, however inadequately, to keep these two together. For example, after a remarkable outpouring of the Spirit on our young church on Mother's Day, 1979, approximately 1,700 people were converted (to Christ).

Our passion still is to imitate the ministry of Jesus in the power of the Spirit. This requires that we follow him out of baptismal waters, through our personal deserts, into the harvest. We want to take the ammunition of the best of conservative Evangelical theology, the best fire power of mainstream Pentecostal practice, fuse them, and hit the biblical target of making and nurturing disciples.[76]

It was January 1982. Fuller Theological Seminary, Pasadena, California. The class, listed in the Fuller course catalog, was simply entitled MC510. Students who signed up for this course, subtitled *Signs, Wonders and Church Growth*, witnessed Professor C. Peter Wagner, the professor of record, introducing his Fuller Evangelistic Association (FEA) associate, John Wimber.

Peter Wagner had employed Wimber in the mid-1970's to work as the director of the FEA after Wimber took one of Wagner's courses at Fuller. By the early 1980s, Wimber had developed quite the reputation as being a pragmatist, which may be one of the primary reasons he suggested the concept of what would eventually become MC510 to Wagner. Keep in mind that Wimber was also pastoring Calvary Chapel Yorba

Linda at the time, where he was practicing in kind what his course material was proposing. Wagner took the bait and they did a dry run as one section of a course that Wagner was teaching on campus in 1981. That then led to the new Missions Course (MC) #510, first offered to Fuller students in January 1982.

On a personal note here, I must tell you that my book editor and publisher, Winn Griffin, attended that first MC510 course at Fuller Seminary and as a result, wrote a paper for Wimber entitled, *"The Invasion of the Kingdom of God into the Kingdom of Satan."* That paper landed Griffin a job as Wimber's writer in the spring of 1982. His first big assignment was to write four full lectures for Wimber to use on a ministry trip scheduled for later that year. Griffin eventually took those lecture notes and the material used in the 1982 MC510 course, refining them into a full text edition that was then used in the 1983 version of the MC510 course at Fuller. In truth, while John Wimber was the face for MC510, it was actually Winn Griffin who melded together Wimber's original material with the works of esteemed biblical scholars such as Charles H. Kraft, Russell Spittler, Mel Robeck, George Ladd, and others, in the development of the 1983 version of MC510 and the MC511 course that followed. All of Griffin's material was later included in Wimber's popular *Signs, Wonders and Church Growth* conferences in 1984 and two best-selling books, *Power Evangelism (1986)* and *Power Healing (1987)*.

Now back to the original MC510 story. After the first MC510 class proved to be so successful, Peter Wagner contacted a friend who was the editor of Christian Life Magazine, suggesting that he dedicate an entire issue of CL magazine to the phenomena surrounding Wimber's course at Fuller. It was this publication in October 1982 that led to the great national visibility Wimber and Vineyard Christian Fellowship of Anaheim enjoyed for years to come.

Who would have guessed back in 1982 that this relatively insignificant seminary course, which raised the simple question, (Is there a direct correlation between Holy Spirit power and effective evangelism?) would go on to cause such a big stir in the

American church? Before the course was cancelled in the late 1980s by a school administration that decided to shy away from the controversy, MC510 became Fuller's most publicized and highly attended course ever offered in the long history of this fine theological seminary. The reason MC510 caught so much flack was it was one of the first attempts ever undertaken by an American theological seminary to actually verify and quantify the role of Holy Spirit power as it relates to the effective growth of the gospel of Christ. Does the use of the "charisma" gifts of the Holy Spirit, (i.e. healing, prophecy, deliverance, tongues, etc.) actually increase the effectiveness of Christian evangelism?

As I see it, one of the primary results of the MC510 course as it was developed into a highly successful conference format, was to give straight-laced evangelicals like me, who generally were very fearful of the excesses found in so many charismatic or Pentecostal circles at the time, a biblically based and theologically sound grounding that encouraged us to be open to the power of the Holy Spirit as we pursued our mission of evangelism across the world. The evangelical no longer had to check his or her mind at the door to be what one author termed an "empowered" evangelical.

As a result, effective evangelism, where a clear presentation of the gospel is given, had now been teamed up with the power of the Spirit, as Wimber states in the quote above, for the first time in the twentieth century! And the results, as I see it, changed everything. Now, pastors and churches, who once withdrew from the excesses of Pentecostalism, were given a digestible and easily reproduced model where the Holy Spirit was not just used for personal edification and Pentecostal giddiness, but was now teamed with a clear presentation of the gospel, bringing people to Christ not only by words, but by works as well. Thus, the phrase "power with a purpose" was coined and as they say in the movies, the rest, my friends, is history.

PRAYER

Father, I thank you, that from time to time, you bring forth men and women who serve you as reformers. Simple and humble individuals who truly love your church, but love the church too much to let it stay the same. Thank you for the way you used John Wimber and others to re-establish a long-lost truth; where Holy Spirit presence and power is linked with the sending commission of Jesus. May we continue in that heritage. For your name's sake. Amen!

QUESTION FOR YOU TO PONDER

- Working with the power gifts of the Holy Spirit (i.e., healing, deliverance, tongues, prophecy, etc.) as he moves in immature believers often brings a self-focused, self-edifying environment. In church life, then, it becomes easier, and often less messy, for pastors to separate Holy Spirit power and presence from Jesus' commission to "go and make disciples." Knowing that it's biblical to fuse the two, how can I stay the course in insisting that my church be made up of a people who are "empowered evangelicals," Spirit-filled and kingdom-directed people who never become so inwardly focused on the power gifts that they lose their outward drive to go into the world to see Jesus save and secure the lost?

So, what is God speaking to you today as you ponder the *Wisdom of Wimber*?

THE "E" WORD

> The groom wants a healthy bride, not some emaciated fashion model who only appears beautiful. Our evangelism and church planting should reflect this optimism: with or without us, Jesus is marrying a big bride and church planting is still the most effective evangelistic tool on the face of the earth.
>
> Our purpose, then, is to evangelize the lost, enfold them in new churches, equip them to exalt Jesus in every area of life, and so expand his kingdom through continuing his ministry. The Association of Vineyard Churches evolved through our desire to do this more effectively by working together to train and oversee pastors and leaders.[77]

Evangelism. The "E" word. The word so many of us in our churches fear. The idea of sharing our faith in Christ with others is a scary endeavor for most of us. Particularly in a society where Christianity is looked at with such cynicism. Over my thirty years in pastoral ministry, I've found that it's so easy for so many of us Christians to settle down into our churches, get warm and cozy, and focus exclusively on caring for one another in the safe and sound settings of our common church life. As a shepherd at heart, if left to my own devices, I can very easily be lulled to sleep caring for the flock and watching over the concerns of those who attend the church I pastor.

Here's the rub. Jesus, the shepherd, was never content to go off with his small flock of followers, removing himself permanently from the rest of the world around him. As I see it, Jesus of Nazareth, the contemplative shepherd, was a full-fledged activist as well.

Let me share a new term I'm coming to truly appreciate: Contemplative Activism. My spiritual director, Dr. Micha Jazz, defines it this way:

Let's remind ourselves that Contemplative Activism combines two ideas, the first one being the essential, yet often lost art of drawing aside with God for prayer and learning how to find Him in every aspect of life. Contemplative experience provides a door to discovering so much more about ourselves, each other, God and His ways.

However there is a danger having ascended the heights through Contemplation, that we may not want to return and make our descent back into the streets of chaos within which we are called to carry out the mission of God. Secondly, therefore, we seek to live out prayer by rolling up our sleeves and serving the needs of the surrounding community. The Contemplative Activist develops the rhythm of ascent and descent in living the Spirit filled life.[78]

A contemplative activist.

Hmm. Come to think of it, maybe that's why I loved being around a man like Wimber.

As I see it, John Wimber was a contemplative activist. He certainly was one of the best worshippers I've ever been around. He seemed to know how to be quiet and wait patiently for the Lord to whisper instructions into his ear. As a man of peace, he seemed to truly love the church he shepherded. He had compassion and warmth for every soul he met, and from my perspective, he could be as fatherly as anyone I've known. John Wimber: a contemplative? Yeah, I'd say he had that side to him.

But there was another part of Wimber. A man who loved the "E" word. An activist, not content to sit on the bench and let the world go to hell in a hand-basket. One who knew very well that Jesus hadn't called the church to gather up their warm fuzzy blankets and hide away in some hidden-away sanctuary, waiting for the Master to return. No, he knew full well that the same flock he shepherded had also been called and commissioned by Jesus to go and "love the hell" out of the rest of the world.

Dr. Jazz defines contemplative activism as learning to develop a "rhythm of ascent and descent in living the Spirit filled life." I like that. So now, as we enter into these next few sessions on evangelism, let this concept of "staying" with Jesus to "go" in his name, lead the way.

PRAYER

Jesus, while I truly love the call to pastoral shepherding, please never allow me to become so comfortable in that role that I forget that we, your church, are all called to go and give away the same good news that has so radically transformed our own lives. Spirit, empower me to become a contemplative activist, one who lives out the rhythms of ascent and descent. For your name's sake. Amen!

QUESTIONS FOR YOU TO PONDER

- As a quiet, reflective man, the "E" word can be so frightening and downright threatening to me. What changes do I need to make in my day-to-day life so that I never lose the call and commission of Christ to "go" in his name to love both the saved and unsaved in the world around me?
- What action steps can I take today to be actively involved in Jesus' advancing kingdom mission to the world?

So, what is God speaking to you today as you ponder the *Wisdom of Wimber?*

"But you, keep your head in all situations, endure hardship, do the work of an evangelist, discharge all the duties of your ministry." (2 Timothy 4:5)

Paul continues to exhort Timothy to fulfill his ministry in the face of hard times, times when many might turn away from the truth. Though others might chase after new truths, Timothy and we are encouraged to keep our heads and endure hardship. Sometimes there is nothing we can do to "fix" the situation. Instead of being surprised and discouraged at difficult days and resistant people, we must learn to be at peace and persevere in our work.

Paul also reminds us along with Timothy to do the work of an evangelist. We all need to be reminded not to become too inward looking so that we forget the people outside the fellowship of the church. These people desperately need to know Jesus and experience his dramatic deliverance and restoration. God wants us to continue to seek out the lost and minister the whole gospel, *words and works*, to them.[79]

In the previous section, I mentioned a new phrase that I'm coming to love: contemplative activism.

As I see it, Wimber was a "contemplative activist" long before anyone had popularized the phrase. Previously, I suggested that Wimber was a very effective evangelist, much like the mature man of God the apostle Paul talks about here in his letter of encouragement to Timothy. But know this. Wimber was not only an effective evangelist, he was also a powerful worshipper, one who loved to practice the fine art of resting in God's presence, waiting on him even when the flesh was yelling to get on with the show.

The long-standing perseverance Paul refers to here in 2 Timothy 4:5 is not the "pull-yourself-up-by-the-boot-straps" kind of faith that someone develops on their own, or by reading a book or two on evangelism. The type of gut-wrenching perseverance Paul is looking for in his young son Timothy, is the unswerving, unwavering certainty of faith that comes only by standing for long periods in the fiery flames of God's presence!

I'm reminded of a quote accredited to the great evangelist, Bill Bright, who once said about effective evangelism, "The best evangelist is one who first talks to God about men before he goes and talks to men about God." The best evangelism is birthed out of the passions of God's own heart for the lost, not our flesh-driven desire to do something nice for the Almighty!

After nearly thirty years in the pastoral ministry, I've learned that it's never adequate to stand in my own strength. Doing kingdom ministry, entering into the work that Jesus commissions his followers to do, is not an easy task. Following the Master into his work can actually kill you. Just look at Jesus. Only three years into the project, and some who once appreciated him, hanging on every word, turned on him and allowed him to be hung on a cross!

So when Paul encourages his young son in the Lord to "keep your head in all situations, endure hardship, do the work of an evangelist, discharge all the duties of your ministry," I'm certain that this was Paul's way of saying to Tim, "Hey, it's a jungle out there, boy. Get your head screwed on straight and the only way you can do that is to sit in God's presence as much as you can!"

That way, when we go out into the world to discharge all the duties of the ministry, we're not giving away *our* stuff, but we're distributing gems of wisdom and pearls of life that have been given to us by the Spirit, as we've lingered in the sweet presence of the Lord.

Enough talk, already.

Gotta go be contemplative, sitting in God's presence for a good piece of time before I go out later today to be the activist Jesus is asking me to be!

PRAYER

Jesus, it's a dog-eat-dog world out there and if I try to do the work of an evangelist out of my own strength, I'm doomed. But if I can learn the unforced rhythms of grace, where I come into your presence and then go out into the world, I know this whole thing of ministry will go much better for me. Holy Spirit, come. For your name's sake. Amen!

QUESTIONS FOR YOU TO PONDER

- Am I trying to discharge the duties of my ministry out of my own strength?
- Am I wearing out under those pressures because I'm talking to men about God before I'm taking time to talk to God about men?
- What needs to change in my schedule so that I become the contemplative activist rather than the activist who occasionally is contemplative?

So, what is God speaking to you today as you ponder the *Wisdom of Wimber*?

As church leaders, we have little control over who shows up in our churches. It would be nice if we could form a "Dream Team" of capable, happy, well-adjusted, disciples who are willing to do anything necessary to conform their lives to the teachings of Christ and his church - and give ten percent of their income.

Sorry, it's not like that…unless you want to have about three people in your church.

Consider the apostles. They had walked with Jesus for three years. They saw him crucified. They stood inside the empty tomb. And yet, when Jesus appeared to them after his (resurrection) these same men had to be commanded by Jesus to "Touch me and see." Why? Because "…they still did not believe." Yet Jesus gave the church to these men!

Pastors and leaders don't have a draft like the NFL. Just because First Baptist had a lousy season last year, doesn't mean they get the first round draft choice of available converts. When all is said and done, the Lord of the harvest adds to our numbers those who are being saved…those whom he chooses.[80]

Remember, Wimber was a church growth advocate. For several years before starting what would eventually become the Vineyard Christian Fellowship in Anaheim, CA, John traveled extensively across the North American continent, talking with pastors and leaders about how to make their churches grow.

In 1975, Wimber met Peter Wagner at a summer course

on church growth held at Fuller Seminary. By the end of the two-week intensive, Wagner knew that Wimber was a church growth practitioner. During the '70s Wagner served as the CEO of Fuller Evangelistic Association (FEA), which was created by Charles E. Fuller in 1933, and he was a professor at Fuller Seminary, which Fuller along with Carl F.H. Henry and Harold Lindsell had created in 1947. Around 1975, Wagner was establishing the Charles E. Fuller Institute of Evangelism and Church Growth and he reached out to Wimber to give direction to the Charles Fuller Institute. Wimber resigned his pastoral position at the Friends Church in Yorba Linda and accepted Wagner's invitation.[81]

During his years at FEA, Wimber worked the church conference circuit, helping pastors from numerous denominations get a better handle on the changing climate of the day and how the church needed to re-think how they were "doing church." In his own testimony, *I'm a Fool for Christ, Who's Fool Are You?*, Wimber told us how he, at the time, believed that he was doing a noble thing (in helping churches grow), but sadly, he was using spiritual gifts uniquely given to him by the Holy Spirit to manufacture growth in a rather secularized way.

For Wimber, "church growth" at its core is something only Jesus can do to his church. As you can see in the quote above, he eventually came to the point of realization that the secularized pursuit of church growth was not something he wanted to be a part of. I recall many times that he told us pastors who were so caught up in the fine art of church growth that if we kept on that track, we'd end up with a "crowd," but never a "church."

Sadly, I believe we're dangerously close to such a state once again in the American church. Statistics today seem to indicate that the only churches in America that are really growing in numbers are the larger mega churches or churches that are specifically geared toward providing all the bells and whistles church goers in our secularized society insist upon having. Like Wimber, I wonder how many actual "churches" exist in America today. Yes, we have "crowds" of people, but as Wimber so succinctly stated, "a crowd is never a church."

In recent years, Willow Creek Church in the Chicago suburbs did an extensive study, evaluating the long-term effectiveness of their "seeker-sensitive" approach to church growth. Without a doubt, Willow Creek had become one of the key models of "successful" church life by countless pastors across America. Yet when their "Reveal" study was released to the public in 2007-2008, the "church growth" world was shaken to the core.[82] The study actually showed what Wimber had projected thirty years earlier. After two solid decades of utilizing a "seeker-sensitive" approach to church growth, the Willow Creek folks sadly reported that their popularized approach to ministry had actually produced very little in the way of true biblical "discipleship" in the people they were attracting to the ministry! Willow Creek had gathered a "crowd," but had not been all that successful in actually forming "a church" of "Christ followers," men and women who would be seen as "obedient disciples" of Jesus of Nazareth.

Yikes!

So as Wimber stated so very long ago, Jesus is the only one who actually grows his church; and even with our best efforts as evangelists and pastors, we must realize that the church growth job truly belongs to Jesus. Our job, on the other hand, is to be obedient care-givers and disciple-makers, equipping the "crowd" (see Ephesians 4:12-13) to become a "church" of disciples who are learning the fine art of following Jesus in a society where much of what we call Christianity is, what my friend, pastoral coach Dave Jacobs calls, "a mile wide but only an inch deep."

My friends, once again, it's time for a shift in the way we measure "success" in church life. In my own life, I've had to be gut-honest with myself. In 2008, when I had over 350 people coming to my church, I was really thrilled with that fact. My wife and I started our little church in Cedar Rapids, Iowa, with 5 couples in 1998. As I was working as fast as my fat-little butt would go, pushing for more church growth, so we could break the 500 barrier, the Lord finally stopped me in my tracks and began dismantling the church I thought was a "church." In 2008, when I was believing myself to be "successful" as a church growth guy, I had 350 people attending my church, but in fact, all I really had at the time was a "crowd" sitting in the seats with a small group of "disciples" doing a lot of the work. Now, don't get me wrong. I'm not saying that the 350 people in our midst in 2008 were only there for selfish reasons. Actually, what I'm saying is that the problem was inside me! It was me, quite honestly, who was looking at these 350 people as a "crowd" and not truly interested in caring for their souls nearly as much as I was building a bigger church on their backs!

So what about you and your church?

Are you caught up, like I was in 2008, with what I previously described as the 3-Bs, where all I really needed to feel "successful" was victory in the 3-B components of (B)uilding size, (B)ucks in the offering, and the number of (B)utts in the seats? If that's you, my friend, I might suggest that you take your own "Reveal" study, like our friends at Willow Creek, and honestly evaluate what you're doing in the name of Jesus. For me, I know it's time to return to some of Wimber's comments that remind me about what's really important when it comes to true "evangelism and church growth" as Jesus sees it.

I invite you to join a reformation in the way you are doing pastoral ministry for the cause of Christ.

PRAYER

Father, as a pastor who truly wants to find "success" in the ministry I do, help me to take my eyes off "church growth" for "church growth's" sake. Allow me to re-visit the biblical components of what truly makes a church "successful" as seen through the eyes of the Master. Let me love each person Jesus adds to the church I shepherd and may I be faithful to my call to love and equip. For your name's sake. Amen!

QUESTIONS FOR YOU TO PONDER

- How am I allowing "church growth" to rule the way I "do" church?
- Am I consumed with growth to such a degree that I've lost perspective on what actually defines a "successful" church?

- What needs to change for the "crowd" I lead to become a "church" I shepherd and equip for Jesus' ministry?

So what is God speaking to you today as you ponder the *Wisdom of Wimber*?

EMBRACING HIS CAUSE

All over the world there are people who have committed themselves to Christ in the sense that they have prayed the prayer, bowed the head, or raised the hand. They want an insurance policy for the life hereafter — but they are not committed to the church! They disdain the church. Watch out for those. You don't want those people around you. Call them to commitment to the church. Our movement is full of people who are uncommitted to the church. They see it as something to merely accommodate them, to meet their needs. They do not see the church as the vehicle for the mission of Jesus. The first and foremost question isn't, "What's in it for me and my family?" but rather, "What's in it for Jesus? What is he going to get out of this?" It's *his* church.

And it also means commitment to his cause. There are a lot of people who are committed to Jesus, and even to his church — but they are not committed to his cause. How do you know that? By looking at the measurements of how they spend their time, energy and money. They don't give any time to evangelism, to ministering, to caring for the poor, to looking after widows. Look at their calendar. Look at their check book. Who are they serving? It looks to me we are often serving everything *but* Jesus, when we look at where our money goes. Where are you really focused? Most people are not focused on Christ and his cause.[83]

At times, when I read Wimber, I have a hard time believing that it was nearly thirty years ago as of this writing that he was saying the things that he was. The quote above is an example.

Sadly, mainline Christianity across North America has, for the most part, deteriorated even further into the "what's in it for me" mentality Wimber talks about here. Statistics show us, at best, that the church is having a hard time remaining culturally current in our ever-changing society, and those churches that are still growing are doing so by two means. First, transfer growth. That's when people grow tired, bored, or frustrated at their current church setting and switch over to another church in town that apparently is doing a better job of meeting specific needs than the first one. Or second, churches grow in our society today by becoming consumer-driven entities, where people are attracted to the church by offering programming that appeals to our modern society.

Just recently, a local TV news reporter here in Cedar Rapids ran a special story on what local churches are doing to keep the under-forty crowd coming to church. One pastor, who obviously doubts the sovereignty of God and the longevity of Jesus' kingdom, said if we don't do something immediately, the church would no longer exist. Another pastor was a bit more to my liking as he sheepishly apologized to the camera for his new approach to Bible studies, where his small group meets in a local bar to study the word over an evening of drinks!

Now please, don't get me wrong. I like a good beer as much as anyone and I do believe that we can't just sit on our proverbial hands while the world goes to hell in a hand-basket. But sadly, it seems that the church of Jesus Christ has now become so weakened in our cause, we'll do just about anything short of something illegal to attract a crowd. And as we discussed earlier in this book, Wimber would often point out to pastors that there is a major difference between gathering a crowd versus shepherding a church!

Could it be that the cause of Christ has fallen into such lowly estate in the eyes of his church, that it's time for a major reformation throughout the body of Christ? Talk about your need for a total makeover! Maybe Wimber pegged it accurately when he said:

> The first and foremost question isn't, "What's in it for me and my family?" but rather, "What's in it for Jesus? What is he going to get out of this?" It's *his* church.

Let's face it folks. I'm a sixty-something recovering 3-B pastor. I don't claim to have any better handle on the things of God than any of you. I'm as frustrated at the current state of the church in North America as you are. Countless books are being written today on how the church needs a seismic shift in the way we're doing church. I concur. But here's the rub. As I see it, it's time to stop coming up with new ideas on how to revive the church so that we'll be the salt and light Jesus wants us to be.

In fact, coming up with new creative ideas on how to remodel the church is what got us in this mess in the first place. Wimber was spot-on right when he said that the church belongs to Jesus. If we want to go on mission as the church of Jesus Christ, we must make sure that, first and foremost, we, the church, are not leading the cause, but that the cause of Christ is *leading* us!

Haven't we spent enough time with new creative ideas of doing church so that the people will come? Stop the madness of gathering leaders in church growth conferences where we discuss yet another set of bigger and better methods of attracting people to our sanctuaries. Back up the truck on the blogs and webinars that promote man-made promotional packages picturing a twenty-first-century church attendee scoring big-time with Jesus with a Budweiser in his hand.

Here's an idea. Let's stop the madness for, let's say, one year. Let's take one year of silence and Sabbath, 365 days of quiet, 12 months of seeking Jesus exclusively on what he might want from his church in this hour. How about if pastors gather in our cities to be silent and reverent for one hour each week? No pep-talks. No BS. No git-r-done attitudes. Just holy silence, giving God time to hit the reset button, so that the cause of Christ can rise to the surface once more.

Well, that's enough preaching to the choir for now. It's time to go back into silence and solitude, where the cause of Christ becomes the main thing while everything else in ministry steps back into obscurity.

PRAYER

Father, I, for one, confess my stupidity of trying over the years to get creative so that I can attract people to my church. In all honesty, Jesus, that's a pretty crappy goal. If indeed, your cause is the primary cause, then my causes have to take a back seat to yours. Holy Spirit, hush my mouth, so that your cause can surface once more. For your name's sake. Amen!

QUESTIONS FOR YOU TO PONDER

- Which creative ministry ideas that I'm working on right now have been birthed out of my cause or the American cause versus coming out of the cause of Christ?
- Where am I focused on attracting people to my creative ideas while ignoring the fact that Jesus may have much better things for me to do, if I'd simply take the extra time to listen?

So, what is God speaking to you today as you ponder the *Wisdom of Wimber?*

A Family - A Hospital - An Army

How many of your people are actually in the army? That is a crucial question. Now, some of the people in the army are actually in the hospital at the same time. (Remember: the church is supposed to be an army, a hospital, and a family.) Sometimes more people are hospitalized than not. People get shot up. Or some people are back in school getting re-trained because something happened that blocked off their ministry. They are out of the army — but that's okay. They aren't absent without leave. They're being retooled to go back in. You need to know that. And they need to know that it's okay to be in the hospital or to just be in the family. But it's *not* okay to live there permanently! Eventually we have to get you fielded because the measurement is not, "I'm hanging out here indefinitely," but rather, "Here are the sheaves, here are the results, here are the works done in your name and in your service." I've read the Book pretty carefully and that's what I think it's all about. We work with people to get them in the army. Constantly disciple.[84]

One of the very first sermons I heard Wimber preach was one entitled, "What is the Holy Spirit Saying to the Church Today?" In it, I recall him doing his very best to convince his listeners that the season we all live in here in America is a time of war. And during a time of war, he added, it never goes well for people who remain oblivious and unconcerned while bombs are dropping out of the sky all around us. I recall him passionately crying out in this sermon that one of the saddest things about the American church of our day is the fact that too many people in the pews are doing their very best to remain civilians in a time of war!

Bingo!

So for Wimber, church was never about gathering in warm,

protected hideaways where well-behaved Christians could tuck their heads up their butts, sing a few songs, and pray that God would bless us while the rest of the world is going to hell in a hand-basket. For Wimber, the church needed to be three distinct things.

First, the church needs to be a family. A place of adoption, where the Father heart of God surrounds his adopted sons and daughters. A home where there is no stranger. A family where outsiders can become insiders and where compassion and mercy are readily available to all who enter in.

Second, the church needs to be a hospital. In all truth, we are all wounded and defective in one manner or another, leaders and lay people alike. And from time to time, it's important that people can come to our church and give the Lord time to do open heart surgery, bind up a gaping wound, or repair a broken arm or leg. Sadly, in this time of war we are in, many are seriously wounded due to "friendly fire," where well-meaning Christians shoot other well-meaning Christians with their hurtful words or actions. A church needs to be a place where healing can occur and where the wounded can be rehabilitated, nursed back into a healthy state of life, and given their uniform in the armed forces of Christ.

Finally, Wimber believed, as stated above, that ultimately the church needs to become a well-trained, well-equipped army. Without a doubt, Satan knows that his time is short and he's holding nothing back in his arsenal of weapons against human-kind. Look around you. Read the newspapers. Watch TV. Peruse Facebook and Twitter. Open your eyes to the war that rages right outside the stained-glass windows of our rose-colored sanctuaries. People are dying. People are suffering. People are full of hate. People are full of hopelessness and despair. People need a Savior. For Wimber, a church body that ignores the state of war and does its very best to remain civilians in a time of war was heresy. And as I see it, it still is.

So as we close this section of our book on the subject of evangelism, let's go back one more time to the words found at Matthew 28:16-20 in the Message:

Meanwhile, the eleven disciples were on their way to Galilee, headed for the mountain Jesus had set for their reunion. The moment they saw him they worshiped him. Some, though, held back, not sure about worship, about risking themselves totally. Jesus, undeterred, went right ahead and gave his charge: "God authorized and commanded me to commission you: Go out and train everyone you meet, far and near, in this way of life, marking them by baptism in the threefold name: Father, Son, and Holy Spirit. Then instruct them in the practice of all I have commanded you. I'll be with you as you do this, day after day after day, right up to the end of the age.

Sadly, there will still be many who will hold back because of the great risk of dying in a time of war. But without a doubt, like Jesus, we need to go right ahead, undeterred, and keep on keeping on making disciples, teaching and training them in everything Jesus gave his first set of disciples. The commission is clear. The war is on. Will we go in his name, right up to the end of the age?

PRAYER

Father, the work of evangelism will never be completed until the day your precious Son splits the skies and returns to consummate his kingdom work here on earth. The job description is clear. The marching orders are unmistakable. Holy Spirit, indwell and empower me to remain faithfully commissioned in your army. For your name's sake. Amen!

QUESTIONS FOR YOU TO PONDER

- What needs to change in our church environment so that the three descriptions of family, hospital, and army are fulfilled in our midst?
- Where am I still trying to remain a civilian in a time of war, hunkering down or hiding away from the commission Jesus has given me?
- What will it look like for me to serve full-time as a soldier in the salvation army of Jesus Christ of Nazareth?

So, what is God speaking to you today as you ponder the *Wisdom of Wimber?*

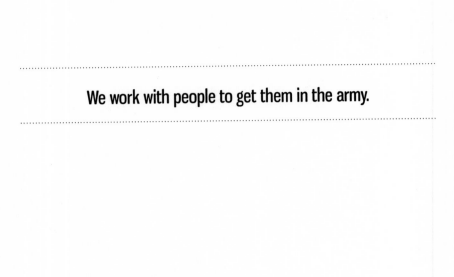

We work with people to get them in the army.

ON DISCIPLESHIP

The first person we often have to disciple is ourselves.

Reproducing Disciples. It's All About Me

The first person we often have to disciple is ourselves. You'll reproduce in kind.

Some of you are in the process of planting a church and are wondering why it isn't happening. It could be one of a thousand variables, but one may be that you are not actually yourself doing the very things you want reproduced in others.[85]

Discipleship, at its very core, is an act of reproduction. And just like parents have little control over the color of their newborn baby's eyes or the lightness or darkness of that child's skin, so it is with discipleship. So much of what results in our discipleship programs has very little to do with what we teach. In all honesty, for Wimber, the quality of your church's discipleship program will have more to do with the character and nature of you, the disciple maker, than anything else.

As Wimber states above, we "reproduce in kind." So, if I am one who cuts corners, looks for loopholes in every situation and never trusts anyone further than I can spit, guess what? Most of the folks who hang around my church will end up looking a lot like that. If I'm a man or woman who gives high regard to others, living a selfless, otherly life, chances are really good that most of those who stay around my church for any length of time will have big hearts for others as well. Make sense?

Quite honestly, it's a scary thing. After thirty years of doing pastoral ministry, I'm both proud to report and also just a bit embarrassed that a lot of the folks who have hung around me for any length of time do actually start looking and acting a lot like me! Now, I truly enjoy that fact when I see a quality in me that I love, but feel a bit sheepish when the opposite happens! Let me give you an example or two.

Sandy and I are worshippers at heart. We're long-time musicians and have always been suckers for a great worship song. In the earliest days of attending Vineyard conferences, I'd always get stuck in the midst of intimate worship and quite often, find myself crying in God's presence. I remember at one big national conference, I found myself so overcome by God's presence in the midst of a Brian Doerksen worship song; I simply had to sit down in my chair and cry my eyes out to God. After some time went by, and the conference had moved on to the announcements or something else, one nice lady sitting near me whispered in my ear, asking if she could pray for me. She obviously thought I was in great pain. I looked up with a big smile and said, "Thanks, but I always do this when God is around!" She gave me a puzzled look and quickly went back to listening to the announcements!

So it is with so many of those who have hung around me over the years. My church will always have a bunch of worshippers who will drop just about everything and anything when someone says, "it's time to worship!"

But just as Wimber says here, the opposite occurs in me and my church as well. You see, I'm also a wee bit shy (or should I say overwhelmingly introverted?) when it comes to outward, expressive evangelism. So there you have it. Over the years, most of the folks who gather around me tend to be the same way. I'm not proud of it, but I do realize that it's true that most of the folks that I disciple over the years will tend to look and act a lot like me! So, good, bad, and ugly, that's the facts, and I have to face that truth and do my best to broaden my own discipleship skills if I want others to do the same!

So as we start out this final section of *The Wisdom of Wimber*, let's remember that real discipleship in our churches begins and ends with you and me, the shepherd of the church. If you want men and women in your church to look like Jesus, you just better be about the business of allowing Jesus to be in full control of your life, first and foremost. If you want folks in your church to be a praying people, you better become one yourself. If you want flaming evangelists, you better not think that by preaching about it long enough, that will make it so. As Wimber states, discipleship is all about "reproducing in kind." I recall in other settings he used to say it this way as well, "quality discipleship is more caught than taught."

So, excuse me folks. Gotta go. As I see it, if I want more people in my church with passionate, obedient hearts for Jesus, I guess I better go practice a bit more on mine!

PRAYER

Father, the mystery of quality discipleship is not all that complicated. If I want more of Jesus in others, I need to get more of Jesus in me. If I want others to have a heart for the poor, I need to work that into my own life. Holy Spirit, come. Work into me, first and foremost, the all magnificent presence of Christ, so that any disciple I work with will receive you as well. For your name's sake. Amen!

QUESTIONS FOR YOU TO PONDER

- So let's be honest. What negative qualities and mannerisms are evident in those around me?
- Once I can identify those issues, am I bold enough to stop accusing others and look inside my own heart to see if many people are actually catching these things from me?
- On the opposite side of the coin, what positive aspects of Christ-likeness can I develop within me so that others can actually catch it from me?

So, what is God speaking to you today as you ponder the *Wisdom of Wimber*?

Years ago as a new Christian, I thought my personal pilgrimage with God was the essence of Christianity. I used to evaluate my maturity over and over again. "Am I growing, Lord?" I remember when I was memorizing Scripture, eventually memorizing about a thousand verses. "Boy," I thought, "I must really be mature. I must really be growing. Look at all these verses that I have memorized." That was how the Bible memory course motivated me: *You want to grow in Christ? Memorize his word.* But in fact I was growing little. I was still biting my wife's head off, yelling at my kids, and doing a thousand things that hurt my relationships. I had lots of verses memorized, but few were worked out in my life.[86]

So what, exactly, defines a disciple?

Over the years, I've always enjoyed asking pastors how they would answer that question. Sadly, as Wimber points out here, there are many in Americanized Christianity who believe a true "disciple of Jesus" is one who can quote the most Scriptures, fill in the most blanks on a bible quiz, and boldly shout down anyone in the room who says the earth might be a bit older than 5,000 years!

In some circles, if it's not Bible knowledge that distinguishes the men from the boys, it's theology. I've sat in some pastoral meetings where it became quite obvious that the one with the most degrees or the one who could spout off the most about his or her viewpoint of God was, indeed, the greatest disciple maker in the room.

But Wimber got it right when he said that something was wrong when he was able to quote a thousand verses, but he was still fighting with his wife, yelling at his kids, while destroying relationships everywhere he went. Kind of reminds me of Paul's letter to the church in Corinth. Remember that one?

Apparently, the folks in that first-century church thought they were doing pretty well at this "discipleship" thing. Yet, when Paul heard some of the details of how these "disciples" were actually living out the gospel of Jesus Christ, he was just about ready to pull his hair out! Look at this shopping list of problems Paul had to address in just his first letter to the "disciples" of Corinth:

1. There were divisions, personality cults, and cliques.
2. Carnality outweighed spirituality.
3. Sexual perversion, fornication, incest, and adultery were commonly practiced and accepted.
4. Pride, worldliness, and materialism reigned within.
5. Church members were taking one another to court.
6. There was rebellion against apostolic authority.
7. There was a failure to discipline members who had fallen into sin.
8. Marital conflict and misunderstanding concerning those who were single were evident.
9. There were abuses of liberty.
10. There were abuses of God's intended roles for husbands and wives.
11. They were failing to properly observe the Lord's Supper.
12. It is not hard to understand how there could also be serious perversion of the spiritual gifts.
13. There were also heresies concerning the resurrection.

Yikes. I wonder how many of these "disciples" in Corinth could quote God's word on a dime and be the first one in line when it came to being highly critical of others in their midst who were not nearly as mature as them?

As I see it, Paul's response to these frightening problems in Corinth tells us quite a lot about how he viewed successful "discipleship." Sadly, in our generation, if we encountered a church with as many problems as the one in Corinth, many leaders today might suggest that more Bible study and verse memorization would address the problems. Or, how about if some of these troubled folks get signed up for our church's Discipleship 101 class? That'll fix it, right?

No. Paul made no programming suggestions at all. What he did say was this:

> If I speak with human eloquence and angelic ecstasy but don't love, I'm nothing but the creaking of a rusty gate. If I speak God's Word with power, revealing all his mysteries and making everything plain as day, and if I have faith that says to a mountain, "Jump," and it jumps, but I don't love, I'm nothing. If I give everything I own to the poor and even go to the stake to be burned as a martyr, but I don't love, I've gotten nowhere. So, no matter what I say, what I believe, and what I do, I'm bankrupt without love. Love never gives up. Love cares more for others than for self. Love doesn't want what it doesn't have. Love doesn't strut, Doesn't have a swelled head, Doesn't force itself on others, Isn't always "me first," Doesn't fly off the handle, Doesn't keep score of the sins of others, Doesn't revel when others grovel, Takes pleasure in the flowering of truth, Puts up with anything, Trusts God always, Always looks for the best, Never looks back, But keeps going to the end. Love never dies. Inspired speech will be over some day; praying in tongues will end; understanding will reach its limit. We know only a portion of the truth, and what we say about God is always incomplete. But when the Complete arrives, our incompletes will be canceled. When I was an infant at my mother's breast, I gurgled and cooed like any infant. When I grew up, I left those infant ways for good. We don't yet see things clearly. We're squinting in a fog, peering through a mist. But it won't be long before the weather clears and the sun shines bright! We'll see it all then, see it all as clearly as God sees us, knowing him directly just as he knows us! But for right now, until that completeness, we have three things to do to

lead us toward that consummation: Trust steadily in God, hope unswervingly, love extravagantly. And the best of the three is love. (1 Cor.13:1-13, The Message).

Hmm. Case closed. Discipleship 101, from Paul's point of view, begins and ends in living and breathing in God's agape love.

PRAYER

Father, forgive us as Christian leaders for taking the word "disciple" and adding so many trappings to it that it becomes so complicated that no one, myself included, could ever arrive at the goal and high standards we've set. Holy Spirit, empower me like Paul, to simplify "discipleship," bringing it down to simple words like faith, hope, and love.. For your name's sake. Amen!

QUESTIONS FOR YOU TO PONDER

- What might it look like if a church community redefined "discipleship" using simple words like the ones found in the thirteenth chapter of Paul's first letter to the troubled "disciples" in Corinth?
- How might an expression like "Live Simply. Love Extravagantly" help simplify "discipleship" in my circle of influence, allowing Jesus to once again lead us into his definition of what a "disciple" truly is?

So, what is God speaking to you today as you ponder the *Wisdom of Wimber*?

DISCIPLESHIP PRE-REQUISITE: WALKING WITH A LIMP

Someone once told me, "I don't trust leaders who don't walk with a limp." Give me a leader who has wrestled with God, and been shown the limitations in his character or make-up.[87]

Wimber's quip, "leaders who walk with a limp," were men and women who have wrestled with God over the years and become damaged goods in the process. They are followers of Christ who know with great certainty that our Redeemer lives, but still wince a bit in pain when asked to tell their faith story.

Sadly, America doesn't seem to like its leaders to limp. Nor does the victorious church of Jesus Christ often recruit men and women who don't look the part of the strong and confident leader. In a society where bigger is always better and more is much more preferable to less, there seems little room today for brokenness or weakness in those who lead. When Wimber was alive, Jesse Ventura, the brawny pro wrestler turned governor of Minnesota, boldly told the press that Christianity is for losers, for people who need a crutch in life, for those who are not strong enough to make it on their own.

You know what, Jesse? You're right.

A quick look at the biblical hall of fame reveals these truths.

Noah was a drunk, Abraham was too old, Isaac was a day-dreamer, Jacob was a liar, Leah was ugly, Joseph was abused, Moses had a stuttering problem, Gideon was afraid, Samson had long hair and was a womanizer, Rahab was a prostitute, Jeremiah and Timothy were too young, David had an affair and was a murderer, Elijah was suicidal, Isaiah preached naked, Jonah ran from God, Naomi was a widow, Job went bankrupt, Peter denied Christ, Jesus' disciples fell asleep while praying, Martha worried about everything, the Samaritan woman was divorced, more than once,

Zaccheus was too small, Paul was too religious, Timothy had an ulcer, and Lazarus was dead!

Hmm.

Somehow, I wonder at times if God actually prefers to use the broken, the least, and the losers? Maybe he knows that if he used the strong and unshakeable ones, those folks, in their pride and arrogance, would take credit for the good stuff that God does in our midst? Maybe in God's economy, he actually takes great joy in doing amazing signs and wonders through what author Henri Nouwen calls "wounded healers."

One of the great mysteries in the life of Wimber was the fact that God used this "simple fat man from Missouri" to heal literally thousands and thousands of people, yet John struggled daily with the lack of healing in his own life. Over the years, Jesus' ministry of healing flowed easily through his hands, so much so at times, I think people were shocked when they found out that Wimber never found much physical healing for his own ailments. Many don't realize that for most of the last ten to fifteen years of his life, Wimber struggled with heart issues, cancer, and some other physical problems that kept him very limited in his ability to travel and minister as he did.

I recall taking him to the airport in June of 1986 after he had just conducted one of the most amazing healing services of which I've ever been a part. As he sat in the front seat of our Dodge Caravan, he looked very tired and pale. He said little as we made our way to O'Hare. Sandy and I could tell that he was exhausted. I excitedly asked him about his many travels and commented on how thrilling it must be to see God move so powerfully everywhere he went. He looked at me with a tired, weary look and said, "Marty, I don't get too excited about traveling these days. I do it primarily because God asks me too." As we drove up to the drop-off area, I retrieved his suitcase from our trunk and offered to take it inside for him. He nodded with a "No, thanks, Marty, I got it" kind of look and Sandy and I still recall seeing this tired, weary warrior shuffling his way through the doors, heading back home to Anaheim so he could preach at his church on Sunday morning.

Ten days later, we heard that he had suffered a heart attack and would be laid up for a few weeks to get his strength back. Our hearts broke for this tireless warrior, a leader with a limp. Over the next eleven years, Wimber would continue his trek of faithfulness, despite the warfare, despite the travel, despite the physical pain. Moving on with Jesus, doing the work of the ministry God had given him with little time to sit at home and rest his weary body for much more than a few days at a time.

As I see it, this is the kind of leader with a limp the American church could use these days. I am thankful that Wimber set the bar for us. I, for one, felt I could trust a leader like him who limped his way through years of faithful service to the Master.

Prayer

Father, thank you for John Wimber, the leader with a limp. And for all those others over the centuries who didn't give up despite their weaknesses and dysfunctions, thank you, Lord. May the Holy Spirit indwell and empower me to keep going despite the times when I feel as though I'm too tired, too unqualified, or too wounded to keep going. For your name's sake. Amen!

Questions for You to Ponder

- So what voices am I listening to today that are telling me that I'm not qualified to be used by God?
- How can I overcome those voices and also help others to believe that despite their brokenness or wounded-ness, the Lord doesn't call the qualified, but qualifies those he calls?

So, what is God speaking to you today as you ponder the *Wisdom of Wimber?*

PEOPLE-KEEPING VS. PEOPLE-PROCESSING

> Some pastors and church leaders mistakenly think ministry is about people keeping. "We got to keep these people coming every Sunday. We got to keep these people giving. We got to keep these people listening to our messages. And most of all, we got to keep these people from going anywhere else." As leaders, we're not in the people keeping business. We're in the people processing business.
>
> Some are like raw lumber still out in the forest when we first meet them. Or they may be in the mill or on their way to the factory. Wherever we find them and in whatever state they're in, our job is to bring them in, and with God's help, make them thoroughly Christian. We need to find out where these people are in this process of maturing and help them along.[88]

Wimber saw the great need for pastors not to "keep" people but freely give away our very best among us, I believe that he was right on with his assessment of Americanized discipleship programs back in the 1980s. As I see it, his words are still spot-on correct today.

Throughout this book, I've been pretty upfront about my own confession of being a 3-B pastor for most of my thirty years in ministry. Who knows, maybe you are as well? Keep in mind that a 3-B pastor is one who measures his or her success (or failure) in ministry by measuring the numbers associated with (B)uilding size, (B)ucks in the offering, and (B)utts in the seats.

Today, as a recovering 3-B pastor, on my way to becoming a contemplative activist, I've joined the ranks of a growing number of pastors and key leaders across North America who have decided to step out of the 3-B traffic, so that we might better align ourselves with Jesus of Nazareth; who, quite honestly, evaluates our effectiveness in ministry much better than anyone else! Sadly, it's taken much of my six decades of life to come to this conclusion, but as they say; better late than never, right?

In my assessment, 3-B pastors are just the kind of pastors Wimber talks about in the quote above as he addresses the problem of "people-keeping" versus "people processing." When a true dyed-in-the-wool 3-B pastor looks at a person who attends his or her church, that individual represents "success" or "failure" based on whether or not the programming of the church can "keep" that person coming to church on Sunday mornings, paying their tithe, and supporting any building projects the church might soon be conducting.

Now some of you will say, "Shame on you, Marty Boller, for saying such a thing," but let me give you my deep-down dirty confession. A confession, from my spot on the playing field, that more pastors across North America need to make.

Let's start with the positive. Yes, most pastors I know, myself included, don't really keep the 3-Bs of (B)uildings, (B)ucks, and (B)utts at the core of our beings. In our hearts, most of us truly love people and we want the best for each person God sends our way. I know many pastors who stay up at night trying to think of more creative ways in assisting people to grow in Christ, becoming more and more of what Wimber talks about here, true followers of Christ who will successfully live mature lives that glorify God.

But, here's the rub.

Because of the underlying pressures to be "successful" in the realm of the 3-Bs, pastors, many times, don't realize that so much of our church programming is actually working against true discipleship. The cold hard truth is that for way too many years at my church, we spent way too little time focusing on how we could aid people in their spiritual growth, while being consumed on how to keep parishioners from slipping out our back door!

As Wimber states above, if pastors would focus more on "processing" the people currently attending our churches instead of sweating bullets on how to "keep" people in our buildings, I think we'd probably see a big increase in our effectiveness toward true discipleship, as it is defined in the New Testament.

I often challenge pastors on this "people-keeping" problem by mentioning to them that Jesus would never be invited to speak at many of our church growth conferences today. Why? Because in today's 3-B culture, breaking the illustrious 200-barrier in church attendance is a pre-requisite for "success" in today's church world. I remind pastors that while Jesus ministered to thousands during his three years of ministry on earth, the Master was not very good at "people-keeping." For heaven's sake, on that day he stood outside Jerusalem, giving his final instructions to his closest associates (see Acts 1), Jesus of Nazareth had gathered only about 120 folks who were faithfully attending his church. Gosh, even the Master, after dying on the cross and rising from the grave, could only muster a church of 120!

So much for people-keeping, huh?

Let's take a honest gut-check, dear fellow pastors and church leaders. How about if we go back to the basics and re-align our church programming so that it truly works toward recruiting, training, building up, and sending out disciples, not just getting and keeping more in our church so that we can feel really successful at growing our church according to 3-B standards?

Anybody up for the 3-B challenge?

PRAYER

Father, I'm quick to confess that I can so easily slip into a "people-keeping" agenda in pastoral ministry. I truly believe that Jesus was not nearly as interested in "keeping" people in church as he was "processing" people for the kingdom of God. Holy Spirit, help me to let go of "keeping" people and allow me the grace to love those who come and go in my church, knowing that your charge to me is to make certain each individual is growing in their personal discipleship, becoming more like Jesus rather than just being another number on my church roles. For your name's sake. Amen!

QUESTIONS FOR YOU TO PONDER

- Where am I allowing the 3-Bs to become my primary measuring stick for "success"?
- Am I too focused on (B)uildings, (B)ucks, and (B)utts in the seats?
- Is it more important for me to close the back door of the church to get our numbers up than it is to make certain each person currently attending is being fully encouraged to grow in their personalized life with Jesus?

So, what is God speaking to you today as you ponder the *Wisdom of Wimber?*

Spiritual children are like natural children. Each one is a surprise. When they come into relationship with Christ, it's like being handed a newborn. You rejoice in the new life, but before long you realize someone has to change the diapers and feed the baby. Someone has to protect the baby. Having babies is hard… but rearing children is where the real work begins.

Likewise, winning people to Christ is exciting, but nurturing and loving them to a state of mature Christian adulthood is hard work. Yet, that's what leaders do.

Unfortunately, everyone who comes to Christ, comes with all kinds of emotional and spiritual baggage. In some cases that baggage will make the job of spiritual formation extremely difficult. They come angry, confused, and bruised. Some of them have been chewed up and spit out by life's difficulties.

Many people come from very nominal church background. They may mistrust the church. They may be individualistic, cocky, and arrogant when they walk in the door.

That's the raw material we deal with.

Furthermore, as leaders we have what seems like an impossible goal. In describing his labor for the church, the apostle Paul writes: "We proclaim him, admonishing and teaching everyone with all wisdom, so that we may present *everyone perfect* in Christ" (Col. 1:28, emphasis added). Paul wasn't interested in presenting everyone reasonably OK in Christ. His goal wasn't to present everyone sort of together in Christ. I've been tempted, at times, to write off some people. But Paul aimed to present everyone he had any degree of influence over perfect in Christ.

Paul said to that end he labored and struggled. But Paul's strength was not his own will, but "his [Jesus'] energy, which so powerfully works in me" (Col. 1:29). As he told the Philippians, "I can do everything through him who gives me strength." When you start working with some of the people the Lord brings to you, you'll need his strength.[89]

A t our church in Cedar Rapids, we say that we put the "fun" in dys-fun-ctional!
Let's be honest, just because I gave my heart to Christ doesn't mean that I've got my life together. For heaven's sake, I made my decision for Jesus years ago when I was just a fat kid with pimples. Now I'm an old fat guy with a receding hairline, and while Jesus has been faithful to me all that time, I still wonder at times if I've made all that much progress toward Christ likeness. What about you? I believe that's why one of Wimber's favorite prayers over the years was, "Father God, help me to grow up before I grow old."

As we get closer to the end of this book, let me give you one of the best life lessons on discipleship that I learned from hanging around Wimber during those early years. As I see it, when it comes to discipleship, we who serve as pastors and leaders in the church have to stop trying to make disciples and followers of Christ.

Stop the presses. What did he just say?

Yes, you read it correctly. We, who serve the church, leaders and shepherds alike, must stop the madness of trying to make disciples, step aside, and allow the true disciple maker to take over a job that, quite honestly, was never ours to pick up in the first place. The world doesn't need any more disciples made by the church. There are way too many of us out there right now stirring pots that Jesus never asked us to touch.

If I read my New Testament correctly, Jesus didn't ask his disciples to go out and reproduce themselves. He commanded them to 1) stay in God's presence until the transforming power and presence of the Holy Spirit overwhelmed (baptized) them; 2) go out in his agape love (not our own strength), loving "the hell" out of people around us; and then 3) bear "witness" (giving testimony) about how the true disciple maker, Jesus of Nazareth, has worked in our lives, transforming us from being "dys-fun-ctional" sinners to becoming much-less "dys-fun-ctional" followers of Christ.

Quite honestly, this concept that we, as followers of Christ, are to go out and make disciples, reproducing ourselves in others, is about as screwy of a notion as one can find. Our role in building the church of Jesus Christ, as Wimber saw it, was to simply become faithful servants in service to the king. The idea that you and I have a ministry is nonsensical. Like he used to tell pastors who would come to him asking for the secret to a successful ministry, "Guys, you don't have a ministry! You'll never have a ministry! There's only *one* ministry out there and it belongs to Jesus!"

I can still see pastors scratching their heads when he would say that to them. Some would eventually get it, but sadly many didn't. Many would come to his "Signs and Wonders and Church Growth" conferences thinking that they could pick up a few pointers from him on how to go back home and make their church start growing. Sadly, many pastors are still going to conferences today with the same mindset.

So, please, my friends. I'll say it as nicely as I can, but I must say it clearly and concisely.

Stop it! Stop trying to build your church. Stop trying to make disciples for Jesus. Stop trying to get your ministry to become successful. Stop trying to assemble a programming format that will keep people in your church.

For heaven's sake, you and I don't have a church! Only Jesus does! And as Wimber used to say to us, "Guys and gals, Jesus wants his church back!"

I guess the questions still remain. Are you and I willing to give the keys of the church back to him? Are we willing to stop making disciples in our own image so that the true disciple maker can have a crack at it instead? Are we willing to become second-bananas to Jesus, allowing him to lead and not us? Are we willing to sit in the passenger seat for a while and let Jesus drive the car where he wants to drive it?

Well, nuff said. I hope I offended you just a bit with my rants and ravings. If I did, I know Wimber, if it were possible, is probably looking down from heaven and smiling. And maybe, just maybe, so is Jesus!

PRAYER

Father, thank you for the reminders you've given me that you never intended for me to be a leader, but simply a first-follower of Christ. Jesus, I lay down my holy pursuit to make disciples for you and allow you to do that as I do my part of simply bearing testimony of all you can do, if we allow you to do it. You, Jesus, are the true disciple maker. I, Lord, am simply your servant. Empower me to do my humble part. For your name's sake. Amen!

QUESTIONS FOR YOU TO PONDER

- What am I doing in ministry today that is actually taking power out of Jesus' hands and placing it in mine?
- Am I indirectly trying to make disciples, build impressive ministries, and do great stuff for Jesus while ignoring the fact that it's the Master alone who makes disciples, builds churches, and gathers people to himself?

So what is God speaking to you today as you ponder the *Wisdom of Wimber?*

The Three Rails of Revival

> We want to engender a deep spirituality in our disciples that rejects a facile triumphal-ism. Disciples realize there will be hard times ahead. The journey we're on is fraught with pain, difficulties, and the onslaughts of the enemy. They also learn we can benefit from trials. From my reading of the Bible (and church history), Christianity doesn't guarantee heaven here on earth. We're going to Heaven – but we may go *through* hell here.[90]

Many of those who study past revivals or spiritual awakenings throughout church history believe that there are three vital components to any successful move of God. When God decides to move powerfully during human events (i.e., send an awakening upon his people), there will tend to be three common threads found within that particular move of God.

I'd like to give you a quick overview of these three components to "revival" and then apply them here to the move of God that birthed the Vineyard movement and so many other Spirit empowered, kingdom-driven churches during the 1980s. When I teach about these three components to spiritual awakening, I like to call them the "Three Rails of Revival." Below, I list the three rails; followed by a short explanation on how these three components were clearly evident in the move of God that John Wimber and others found themselves being a part of in the 1980s and beyond.

Rail #1: A rock-solid Theology that recovers an ancient God-Truth

Every legitimate work of revival begins in the recovery and restoration of a long lost, ancient truth about God, a truth that is solidly grounded in God's unchanging word. In the case of Wimber and the move of God's Spirit in the 1980s, this recovered theology based out of God's word was called "kingdom theology."

261

This worldview, which is solidly established throughout the New Testament text, allows followers of Christ to hold onto and experience the amazing promises of God (kingdom theology would call this "the future breaking in on this present age"), while also being honest with the fact that we still live in a "time between the times" when all suffering has not yet ceased, people still die from diseases, and troubles still exist in the daily lives of Christians and non-Christians alike. Kingdom theology would call this age where Christ has already come, but suffering still exists as "living in the not yet of God's promises." Wimber's quote above encapsulates "the now but the not yet" worldview of kingdom theology, where disciples of the Master are encouraged to hold onto the unshakeable promises of healing and hope from the gospels, while still being totally honest with that fact that we will always live in a difficult world of suffering and pain until the day Jesus makes his second return to earth a reality.

RAIL #2: A SIMPLE AND EASILY REPRODUCIBLE METHODOLOGY THAT COMPLIMENTS THE RECOVERED THEOLOGY (RAIL #1)

The move of God Wimber and others were involved in the 1980s was pegged, by some, as the Third Wave of the Holy Spirit. The first wave, occurring in the earliest part of the twentieth-century and carrying through into the 1950s, was the Pentecostal movement. This was a world-shaking phenomenon that many believe rivaled the outpouring of God's power found in the Book of Acts. A second wave of the Spirit in the twentieth-century actually began in Catholic circles in the early 1960s and swept through the Protestant church throughout the late 60s and 70s. Some called it the Jesus Movement, a sweeping move of God, which touched thousands of young people during this time, birthing a whole new church culture across North America. Most of what we now call "Christian pop music" was birthed during this time frame. This second great move of the Spirit is sometimes better known by most church historians as the Charismatic movement.

The Third Wave was called such by some because they saw it as a third major move of the Holy Spirit in one century; something unprecedented in church history. While there were many men and women who contributed to this move of God, John and Carol Wimber and the Vineyard movement were instrumental in bringing much of the reformation during this time. As I see it, the Pentecostal and Charismatic movement had stirred great interest in the Spirit, but it also brought a large divide between those receptive to the Spirit and those who thought that much of the activity in Pentecostal and Charismatic circles had become too excessive, thus, distancing itself from many practical truths found in Scripture. This "third" move of the Holy Spirit in the 1980s, and John Wimber particularly, had an amazing ability to bring a well-thought out theology and methodology to the things of the Spirit, thus giving a lot of skeptical pastors a comfortable place to land when it came to opening themselves up to the work of the Holy Spirit in both their personal lives and in the life and ministry of their churches. The ten basics we've been covering throughout this book formed much of the methodology many pastors needed to step into the sometimes uncertain and often choppy waters of following the Holy Spirit wherever he might go.

RAIL #3: HOLY SPIRIT POWER AND PRESENCE

Both the Bible and church history show us that no spiritual awakening, revival, or renewal of God's people is something humankind can do for themselves. It's evident to those who study revival that it's only the on-going power and presence of God, which can indwell and empower any move of the Spirit in people's hearts.

I spent a lot of my sixty-plus years in Chicago. Folks who live in the Windy City know what I'm referring to when I say the "Three Rails of Revival" is similar to the "L": the three-railed public transportation system that weaves its way through the streets of Chicago. Revival, you see, consists of two basic rails on which the "awakening" train runs. These two solid ribbons of steel (Theology and Methodology) are established by godly men and women who are listening carefully to God and are determined to keep the basic truths of a new movement Christ-centered, kingdom driven and biblically sound. Take away one of these two rails and you have, of course, a train wreck! But just as it is with the

"L" in Chicago, while these two iron rails are vital in keeping the train on its tracks, absolutely nothing will happen unless the train is connected to the electrified third rail that runs between the two outer rails. When the "L" train establishes contact with this middle electrified rail, the whole system works, delivering people wherever they need to go throughout the Windy City. But turn the electricity of that third rail off and passengers are stuck, going nowhere fast. So it is with the third rail of revival. When the Holy Spirit power is on, the awakening spreads. Turn off the power, and the movement comes to a screeching halt. Pastors familiar with Third Wave experiences with the Holy Spirit reasoned that this is why Jesus told his followers to stay in Jerusalem until "the third rail" (i.e., the Holy Spirit) was established within them. So it is with every move of God since then and will be until the end of time.

We can have both a biblically based theology and a well-tuned system of methodology in their proper places, but if little or no power is brought into the church through the indwelling and empowerment of the Holy Spirit, we are left with a beautiful edifice that looks very effective on paper, but sadly, of little or no use to God's kingdom purposes in our world.

So it is with so much of the church across North America today. We can read and reflect upon the Scriptures, seeing how the first century church was able to accomplish all it did. We gaze at church history and see how Francis of Assisi, Martin Luther, John Wesley, Billy Graham, and yes, even John Wimber, were used by God to touch past generations. But here's my question.

Who, in our midst, will embrace the "Three Rails of Revival" and allow God to, once again, pour his Spirit out upon his church, awakening our souls and sending the first major move of God for the twenty-first century? My heart tells me that the fields are ripe for renewal and revival. Maybe you, my dear reader, while reflecting on the ten truths that Wimber once held dear, might be one that God uses in this generation to light the fires of awakening once more!

PRAYER

Father, it's my prayer that awakening will once again come to your church and to your world. A powerful presence of God that is so evident in the lives of your followers that even the skeptics will look at the fruit of that awakening and admit that only Jesus could do such amazing things in the hearts and minds of men and women. You've done it before, Lord. I pray that you'll do it once again! For your name's sake. Amen!

QUESTIONS FOR YOU TO PONDER

- What long lost God-truths need to be recovered in our generation?
- What simple and easily reproduced methodology might be birthed so that millions can easily access the kingdom of God and all Jesus has for us today?
- Finally, what might we do to clear the way for the Holy Spirit to indwell and empower all Jesus desires to do in this generation? Is there anything I'm doing to shut down the power or derail the locomotive of God-awakening in my life?

So, what is God speaking to you today as you ponder the *Wisdom of Wimber*?

When God decides to move powerfully during human events (i.e., send an awakening upon his people), there will tend to be three common threads found within that particular move of God.

CONCLUSION

A prayer I pray often is: "Lord let me grow up, before I grow old.

Maturity does not automatically come with the passage of years. Some of the people we work with may be spiritually much younger than their chronological age. A prayer I pray often is: "Lord let me grow up, before I grow old."[91]

Well, there you have it.

In *The Wisdom of Wimber: As I See It*, I have set out ten over-arching themes. Sixty-three different quotes with sixty-three entries, giving my commentary on words I will never forget. Without a doubt, John Wimber made one huge impact on my life. After reading this book, I pray his words might impact you as deeply as well.

They say it takes a generation or so to assign "greatness" to a man's life. In his day, John Wimber was influential indeed. But as I see it, it's only now, nearly twenty years after his untimely death in 1997 that his contributions to Christianity will begin to shine like twinkling stars in the midst of darkened sky.

In all truth, after giving his life to Christ, this pot-smoking, drug-using hippie from the Los Angeles basin lived a pretty good existence. Along with his wife, Carol, John Wimber was used by Jesus to touch thousands upon thousands of lives, encouraging so many of us to get closer to Jesus, believe everything in the Bible was still true today, and maybe most importantly, taught us that all of us could be fruitful ministers of the gospel, if we only would take the risk of doing just that. Not bad for a simple fat guy from Missouri whose primary goal for most of his life was just to get to heaven!

There are so many other great stories and memorable quotes coming from the Wimber archives, I suggest that you pop over to wimber.org and order up a bunch of books, DVDs, and other assorted resources, bringing John's wisdom into your current existence. My humble suggestion is for you to grab a copy of John's testimony

DVD called "I'm A Fool For Christ, Whose Fool Are You?" and laugh your way through ninety minutes of powerful God-stories told by one who just might have been one of the best story-tellers I've ever heard.

In closing this book, I thought I'd share with you John's taxi cab story. Over the years, I've seen it published or referred to by other well-known pastors. My friend, Christy Wimber, recently published it in the book *Everyone Gets to Play*. Actually, I'm not surprised that the story keeps popping up here and there. Without a doubt, it demonstrates for so many today how the Americanized church tends to stray from the gospel, and illuminates the great need in the North American church to get back to the basics when it comes to 'doin' the stuff' that Jesus commissioned us to do.

So, without further ado, let me share with you, in closing, John's famed taxi cab story:

> Years ago in New York City, I got into a taxi cab with an Iranian taxi driver, who could hardly speak English. I tried to explain to him where I wanted to go, and as he was pulling his car out of the parking place, he almost got it by a van that on its side had a sign reading "The Pentecostal Church." He got really upset and said, "That guy's drunk." I said, "No, he's a Pentecostal. Drunk in the spirit, maybe, but not with wine." He asked, "Do you know about church?" I said, "Well I know a little bit about it; what do you know?" It was a long trip from one end of Manhattan to the other, and all the way down he told me one horror story after another that he'd heard about the Church. He knew about the pastor that ran off with the choir master's wife, the couple that had burned the church down and collected the insurance – every horrible thing you could imagine.
>
> We finally get to where we are going, I paid him, and as we're standing there on the landing, I gave him an extra-large tip. He got a suspicious look in his eyes – he'd been around, you know. I said, "Answer me this one question." Now keep in mind, I'm planning on witnessing to him. "If there was a God and He had a church, what would it be like?" He sat there for a while making up his mind to play or not.
>
> Finally he sighed and said, "Well, if there was a God and He

had a church – they would care for the poor, heal the sick, and they wouldn't charge you money to teach you the Book."

I turned around, and it was like an explosion in my chest. "Oh, God." I just cried; I couldn't help it. I thought, "Oh Lord, they know. The world knows what it's supposed to be like, and we as the Church don't get it most of the time!"[92]

Care for the poor.
Heal the sick.
Teach the Book with no strings attached.

Hmm. Sounds pretty simple, yet radical, doesn't it? As I see it, this three-pronged game plan worked well for both the Master (two thousand years ago) and John Wimber (a generation ago). Anybody wanna try it in this generation?

PRAYER

Father, I thank you for the life and ministry of John Wimber. While not a saint, he was truly a man who did his very best to practice the presence of God, responding in obedience to anything and everything he sensed you asking him to do. While at times, people thought him to be the fool, I, for one, believe that he modeled the Christian life just about as well as anyone I've ever known. May I do half as well as he did. For your name's sake. Amen!

QUESTIONS FOR YOU TO PONDER

- So what needs to change in my life and ministry so that it reflects the three-pronged wisdom spoken by that taxi cab driver in New York City? Care for the poor. Heal the sick. Teach the Book with no strings attached. What practical steps can I take today to move my work for Jesus in that direction, for his name's sake?

So, what is God speaking to you today as you ponder the *Wisdom of Wimber*?

Meet the Author: Marty Boller.

As I mentioned earlier, I identify myself as a recovering 3-B pastor on my way to becoming a contemplative activist.

- Let me give you a quick bio. I'm from Iowa (a true Hawkeye at heart) and am married to Sandy (Unrue) Boller, who is from Indiana and hails herself as a Northwestern Wildcat. In the true spirit of the radical middle, we met in the middle…Illinois. We both grew up in mainline denominational churches, experiencing the power and presence of God from a very early age in life. Both of us were music education majors in college and we met as music teachers in Wheeling, IL, a blue-collar community in the northwest suburbs of Chicago. We married in Skokie, IL in 1975. Now all these years later, we have four marvelous adult children (all married to wonderful spouses), with six beautiful grandchildren and counting.

- In 1976, a group of twenty or so friends formed what has now become the Vineyard Church of Evanston, IL. While serving during the mid-1980s as volunteer children's ministry leaders at the church (known then as Christ Church of the North Shore), Sandy and I were greatly impacted by John Wimber and the Vineyard movement. Wimber made several important visits to our church in the mid-1980s, transforming just about everything we knew about worship, church life, the kingdom of God, and practicing the presence of God.

- Moving to Iowa in 1987, Sandy and I founded the first Iowa City Vineyard in 1988. By the fall of 1991, I had joined the pastoral staff of River of Life Ministries under the direction of Pastor Francis Frangipane. As an associate pastor there, I led such city-wide ministries as March for Jesus and Promise Keepers. In 1995, I was hired onto the national staff of Promise Keepers to serve full-time as an area manager for Iowa and several other Midwestern states. It was during this season, I had the extreme joy of working with followers of Christ who represented the full spectrum of the Christian faith.

- In 1997, God began pouring out for us a vision for a new church community in Cedar Rapids. With a rich blessing from River of Life, Father's House Vineyard Church started as a small group of 5 couples meeting in our home in January, 1998. In October, the church held our first public worship service in a storefront location in downtown Cedar Rapids. By the following summer, we had already outgrown our first meeting place. After a short four-year stint in a remodeled downtown theatre, we found a larger, more permanent facility in SW Cedar Rapids, remodeling a former bar into a contemporary setting for worshipping and serving Jesus.

Today, my wife, Sandy, and I are choosing, after 30 years in pastoral ministry, to leave the pressures of the 3-Bs behind us, joining with others who are looking to simplify their walk with Jesus, aligning with what some say is a global movement toward contemplative activism. Simply put, a Christ-centered contemplative activist desires to step out of the busy traffic of what one author calls "Church, Inc." and better align themselves with Jesus of Nazareth, who quite honestly, evaluates our effectiveness in ministry much better than anyone else!

We are now serving the larger body of Christ as contemplative coaches to pastors & spiritual directors to all who are looking for Christ-centered direction in their lives. We are available for individual, spiritual direction, group direction, and retreats, workshops, and seminars focused on helping individuals, groups, and churches focus on the themes of contemplative activism.

I invite you to join us at www.pastorboller.com.

Care for the poor.

Heal the sick.

Teach the Book with no strings attached.

BIBLIOGRAPHY AND ENDNOTES

BIBLIOGRAPHY

Barrett, David B., George T. Kurian, and Todd M. Johnson. *World Christian Encyclopedia: A Comparative Survey of Churches and Religions in the Modern World.* Oxford; New York, NY Oxford University Press, 2001.

Boller, Marty, "As I See It," http://www.pastorboller.com (accessed August 15 2014).

brillig.com, "U.S. National Debt Clock," brillig.com http://www.brillig.com/debt_clock/ (accessed August 12 2014).

Buettner, Dan. *The Blue Zones: Lessons for Living Longer from the People Who've Lived the Longest.* Washington, D.C.: National Geographic, 2008.

_____, "How to Live to Be 100," TED. www.bluezones.com/2009/09/ted-talks-dan-buettner-how-to-live-to-be-100/.

Faris, Bill. "Vineyard-at-Home E-Mail Newsletter." Fall 2013.

Jackson, Bill. *The Quest for the Radical Middle.* Cape Town: Vineyard International Publishing, 1999.

Jazz, Micha, "Axiom Rhythm and Resources Handbook," Axiom www.christouraxiom.com/wp-content/uploads/2013/09/AXIOM_BOOK_2-Rhythm_and_Resources-eBook-1.pdf (accessed July 24 2014).

Krejcir, Richard J., "Statistics and Reasons for Church Decline (Research from 1998 to 2006)," The Francis A. Schaeffer Institute of Church Leadership Development www.churchleadership.org/apps/articles/default.asp?articleid=42346&columnid=4545 (accessed June 3 2014).

Marshall, I. H., *New Bible Dictionary.* Grand Rapids, MI:InterVarsity Press, 1996.

Moll, Rob, "Scrooge Lives!," www.christianitytoday.com/ct/2008/december/10.24.html?start=1 (accessed June 3 2014).

Peterson, Eugene. *The Contemplative Pastor.* Grand Rapids, MI: William B. Eerdmans Publishing Company, 1989.

_____. *A Long Obedience in the Same Direction: Discipleship in an Instant Society*. Grand Rapids, MI: InterVarsity Press, 2000.

Rainey, Russ, "Willow Creek Reveal Study – a Summary," The Christian Coaching Center http://www.christiancoaching-center.org/index.php/russ-rainey/coachingchurch2/ (accessed August 17 2014).

Sjogren, Steve. *The Perfectly Imperfect Church: Redefining the "Ideal" Church*. Loveland, CO: Group Publishing Inc., 2002.

Smith, Christian, Michael O Emerson, and Patricia Snell. *Passing the Plate: Why Americans Don't Give Away More Money*. London: Oxford University Press, 2008.

Swindoll, Charles R., "Hilarious Generosity," Insights for Living Ministries http://www.insight.org/store/hilarious-generosi-ty-mng.html (accessed August 12 2014).

Wagner, C. Peter. *How to Have a Healing Ministry without Making Your Church Sick!* Ventura, CA: Regal Books, 1988.

Wimber, Carol. "Worship: Intimacy with God." Equipping the Saints. Vol. 1, No. 1, (1987).

Wimber, Christy, "John Wimber," wimber.org http://www.wimber.org/john-wimber/ (accessed August 22 2014).

Wimber, John. "Ministering the Compassion of Jesus." First Fruits. Vol. 2, No. 3, (1985).

_____. "Push Forward the Kingdom." First Fruits. Vol. 2, No. 6, (1985).

_____. "The Cost of Commitment" (DVD). Harrogate, England: Vineyard Ministries International, 1987.

_____. "Fellowship: Strength in Troubled Times." Equipping the Saints. Vol. 1, No. 2, (1987).

_____. *I'm a Fool for Christ. Whose Fool Are You?* (DVD). Anahiem, CA: Vineyard Ministries International, 1987.

_____. "Worship: Intimacy with God." Equipping the Saints. Vol. 1, No. 1, (1987).

_____. "The Cross." Equipping The Saints. Vol. 2, No. 2, (1988).

_____. "Releasing Gifts in Us." Equipping the Saints. Vol. 7, No. 4, (1993).

_____. "A Leadership Shopping List." Vineyard Reflections. Vol. January/February, (1994).

_____. "Leadership and Followership." Equipping the Saints. Vol. Third Quarter, (1995).

_____. "The Church Jesus Builds." Voice of the Vineyard. Vol. Spring, (1997).

_____. "The Seven Constants of Church-Planting." Cutting Edge. Vol. 2, No. 1, (1998).

_____. *Everyone Gets to Play*. Boise, ID: Ampelon, 2006.

_____. *The Way in Is the Way On*. Boise, ID: Ampelon, 2006.

Wimber, John, and Kevin Springer. *Power Healing*. San Francisco, CA: Harper & Row, 1987.

www.pewforum.org, "Appendix B: Methodology for Estimating Christian Movements," www.pewforum.org http://christianity.about.com/gi/o.htm?zi=1/XJ&zTi=1&sdn=christianity&cdn=religion&tm=45&f=10&tt=65&bt=2&bts=2&zu=http%3A//www.pewforum.org/uploadedFiles/Topics/Religious_Affiliation/Christian/ChristianityAppendixB.pdf (accessed August 22 2014).

ENDNOTES

1. We suggest that you visit www.wimber.org for more on John Wimber, hosted by our friends, Christy & Sean Wimber.

2. John Wimber, *I'm a Fool for Christ. Whose Fool Are You? (DVD)* (Anahiem, CA: Vineyard Ministries International).

3. John Wimber, "The Cross," *Equipping The Saints* 2, no. 2 (1988): 4, 7.

4. Wimber, *I'm a Fool for Christ. Whose Fool Are You? (DVD)*.

5. Bill Jackson, *The Quest for the Radical Middle* (Cape Town: Vineyard International Publishing, 1999), 81.

6. Wimber, *I'm a Fool for Christ. Whose Fool Are You? (DVD)*.

7. Jackson, *The Quest for the Radical Middle*, 53.

8. Christy Wimber, "John Wimber," wimber.org http://www.wimber.org/john-wimber/ (accessed August 22 2014).

9. John Wimber, *The Cost of Commitment (DVD)* (Harrogate, England: Vineyard Ministries International).

10. Wimber, *I'm a Fool for Christ. Whose Fool Are You? (DVD)*.

11. John Wimber, "The Church Jesus Builds," *Voice of the Vineyard*. Spring (1997): 13.

12. John Wimber, "A Leadership Shopping List," *Vineyard Reflections*. January/February (1994): 2.

13. John Wimber, "Push Forward the Kingdom," *First Fruits* 2, no. 6 (1985): 5.

14. Eugene Peterson, *A Long Obedience in the Same Direction: Discipleship in an Instant Society* (Grand Rapids, MI: InterVarsity Press, 2000). This reference is to the Second Edition, the 20th Anniversary edition. Peterson wrote this book originally in 1980.

15. Wimber, "Push Forward the Kingdom," 5-6.

16. Wimber, "The Church Jesus Builds," 12.

17. John Wimber, "Worship: Intimacy with God," *Equipping the Saints* 1, no. 1 (1987): 5.

18. Carol Wimber, "Worship: Intimacy with God," *Equipping the Saints* 1, no. 1 (1987): 4-5.

19. Wimber, "Worship: Intimacy with God," 5,13.

20. Ibid., 13.

21. Ibid.

22. *New Bible Dictionary*, I. H. Marshall. "Worship."

23. Wimber, "Worship: Intimacy with God," 13.

24. Ibid.

25. Wimber, "A Leadership Shopping List," 2.

26. John Wimber, "Releasing Gifts in Us," *Equipping the Saints* 7, no. 4 (1993): 4, 7.

27. Ibid., 5.

28. Ibid., 4-5.

29. Ibid., 5.

30. Ibid., 6.

31. John Wimber, "Fellowship: Strength in Troubled Times," *Equipping the Saints* 1, no. 2 (1987): 5.

32. Ibid., 4.

33. Bill Faris, "Vineyard-at-Home E-Mail Newsletter," Fall 2013.

34. Wimber, "Fellowship: Strength in Troubled Times," 4.

35. Dan Buettner, *The Blue Zones: Lessons for Living Longer from the People Who've Lived the Longest* (Washington, D.C.: National Geographic, 2008).

36. Dan Buettner, "How to Live to Be 100," TED. www.bluezones.com/2009/09/ted-talks-dan-buettner-how-to-live-to-be-100/.

37. Wimber, "Fellowship: Strength in Troubled Times," 4.

38. Richard J. Krejcir, "Statistics and Reasons for Church Decline (Research from 1998 to 2006)," The Francis A. Schaeffer Institute of Church Leadership Development www.churchleadership.org/apps/articles/default.asp?articleid=42346&columnid=4545 (accessed June 3 2014).

39. Wimber, "Fellowship: Strength in Troubled Times," 5.

40. John Wimber, "Leadership and Followership," *Equipping the Saints* Third Quarter, (1995): 6, 8.

41. John Wimber, "The Seven Constants of Church-Planting," *Cutting Edge* 2, no. 1 (1998): 3.

42. John Wimber, "Ministering the Compassion of Jesus," *First Fruits* 2, no. 3 (1985): 3-4.

43. Charles R. Swindoll, "Hilarious Generosity," Insights for Living Ministries http://www.insight.org/store/hilarious-generosity-mng.html (accessed August 12 2014).

44. Wimber, "Ministering the Compassion of Jesus," 4.

45. Ibid.

46. brillig.com, "U.S. National Debt Clock," brillig.com http://www.brillig.com/debt_clock/ (accessed August 12 2014).

47. Christian Smith, Michael O Emerson, and Patricia Snell, *Passing the Plate: Why Americans Don't Give Away More Money* (London: Oxford University Press, 2008).

48. Rob Moll, "Scrooge Lives!," www.christianitytoday.com/ct/2008/december/10.24.html?start=1 (accessed June 3 2014).

49. Wimber, "Ministering the Compassion of Jesus," 4.

50. Wimber, "A Leadership Shopping List," 1-2.

51. John Wimber and Kevin Springer, *Power Healing* (San Francisco, CA: Harper & Row, 1987), xix.

52. Ibid., 55.

53. Ibid., 199.

54. Eugene Peterson, *The Contemplative Pastor* (Grand Rapids, MI: William B. Eerdmans Publishing Company, 1989), 65-66.

55. Wimber and Springer, *Power Healing*, 199.

56. Ibid., 204.

57. Ibid., 211.

58. Ibid., 235.

59. Wimber, "The Church Jesus Builds," 10-11.

60. Ibid., 12.

61. Ibid.

62. Wimber, "The Seven Constants of Church-Planting," 3.

63. Wimber, "Push Forward the Kingdom," 6.

64. Ibid., 4.

65. John Wimber, *Everyone Gets to Play* (Boise, ID: Ampelon, 2006), 118.

66. Ibid., 35.

67. John Wimber, *The Way in Is the Way On* (Boise, ID: Ampelon, 2006), 27, 29.

68. David B. Barrett, George T. Kurian, and Todd M. Johnson, *World Christian Encyclopedia: A Comparative Survey of Churches and Religions in the Modern World* (Oxford; New York, NY Oxford University Press, 2001).

69. www.pewforum.org, "Appendix B: Methodology for Estimating Christian Movements," www.pewforum.org http:// christianity.about.com/gi/o.htm?zi=1/XJ&zTi=1&sdn=christia nity&cdn=religion&tm=45&f=10&tt=65&bt=2&bts=2&zu=ht tp%3A//www.pewforum.org/uploadedFiles/Topics/Religious_ Affiliation/Christian/ChristianityAppendixB.pdf (accessed August 22 2014).

70. Wimber, "A Leadership Shopping List," 5.

71. Wimber, "The Church Jesus Builds," 12.

72. Public Domain.

73. Wimber, "Fellowship: Strength in Troubled Times," 4-5.

74. Steve Sjogren, *The Perfectly Imperfect Church: Redefining the "Ideal" Church* (Loveland, CO: Group Publishing Inc., 2002).

75. Marty Boller, "As I See It," http://www.pastorboller.com. (accessed August 15 2014).

76. Wimber, "The Church Jesus Builds," 11-12.

77. Ibid., 12-13.

78. Micha Jazz, "Axiom Rhythm and Resources Handbook," Axiom www.christouraxiom.com/wp-content/uploads/2013/09/ AXIOM_BOOK_2-Rhythm_and_Resources-eBook-1.pdf (accessed July 24 2014).

79. Wimber, "Push Forward the Kingdom," 6.

80. Wimber, "Leadership and Followership," 5.

81. C. Peter Wagner, *How to Have a Healing Ministry without Making Your Church Sick!* (Ventura, CA: Regal Books, 1988), 47-48.

82. Russ Rainey, "Willow Creek Reveal Study – a Summary," The Christian Coaching Center http://www. christiancoachingcenter.org/index.php/russ-rainey/ coachingchurch2/ (accessed August 17 2014).

83. Wimber, "The Seven Constants of Church-Planting," 2.
84. Ibid., 3.
85. Ibid.
86. Wimber, "Fellowship: Strength in Troubled Times," 4-5.
87. Wimber, "A Leadership Shopping List," 4.
88. Wimber, "Leadership and Followership," 5.
89. Ibid., 5-6.
90. Ibid., 8.
91. Ibid.
92. Wimber, *Everyone Gets to Play*, 117-118.

CPSIA information can be obtained at www.ICGtesting.com
Printed in the USA
BVOW01s0714201214

380010BV00002B/207/P

9 781935 959557